THE HISTORY OF
HIGHGATE
GOLF CLUB

THE HISTORY OF
HIGHGATE
GOLF CLUB

John Chaumeton

First published in 2004 by
Corpus Publishing Ltd
Unit 5, The Marina, Harbour Road,
Lydney, Glos, GL15 5ET, UK.

ISBN 1 903333 16 4

Printed and bound in Singapore
by Kyodo Printing Co

10 9 8 7 6 5 4 3 2 1

CONTENTS

ACKNOWLEDGEMENTS

My thanks must go firstly to the Church of England Record Office, where the staff were always most helpful. Luckily it is their policy not to destroy any original files, so I was able to spend many hours reading how the Club came to lease the land at Fortis Green and later at Highgate.

I was given much help by the Hornsey Historical Society and also the Highgate Literary & Scientific Institute, particularly their archivist, Gwynydd Gosling.

Phillip Truett, a leading light in the British Golf Collectors' Society, has been a constant source of help and material.

My thanks to David Dutton for obtaining and supplying the Ordnance Survey maps.

I am indebted to John Titterton, who died in 2000, but who first played golf at Highgate in 1914 and with whom I had a long and interesting correspondence, culminating in a meeting at Edinburgh in 1999. I am also indebted to Arthur Andress, who first caddied at Highgate in 1908, and who died a few years ago. Both had total recall.

I thank Ian Wallace, John Bracewell, John Scott, Bill Jack and Neville Jones for their contributions. The South Bedfordshire Golf Club was very helpful in providing information and newspaper cuttings about the Club in the early years.

Much help was provided by Rodney Wilkinson, who joined the Club in the thirties, and whose father was Captain in 1934. The watercolours of the course he painted in the summer of 1944, when on leave from the Army, were a great find.

I am indebted to the following organisations for their kind permission to use their material: Aero Films Ltd, *The Hampstead and Highgate Express*, *The Hornsey Journal, Golf Illustrated*, Landmark Information Group Ltd and Ordnance Survey for permission to use its maps.

I am very grateful to Amanda Attenburrow for permission to use her artist's impression of the Bishop's Hunting Lodge.

I should also mention a former member of the Club, Jim Mathie, who, entirely off his own bat, started in the eighties to collect information about the Club. His early researches were most helpful. Various members of the Club provided me with information of one sort and another, much of it insightful. I should not overlook my wife, Ann, who was always most tolerant and helpful with my researches.

If I have overlooked anyone, my apologies.

Finally, I wish to thank fellow member Nick Kent, who has acted as my editor and whose professional help has been vital. Most importantly, he has given me great encouragement in what, at times, has been a rather daunting venture.

To one and all, my heartfelt thanks.

John Crammers, Highgate,
July 2003

*F*OREWORD

This book is a celebration of the first century in the life of a very special golf club.

Highgate may not have the national reputation of a Wentworth or a Sunningdale, but that is surely part of its charm.

It remains one of London's best-kept secrets. How many times have you heard these words from a first-time visitor to our Club: "I had no idea that there was a golf course here!"?

It is nothing short of a miracle that 81 acres in the middle of one of the most expensive residential areas on earth has survived as green and pleasant land for the recreation of those that have been afflicted by a passion for golf.

One of the fascinating facts unearthed during John Chaumeton's delvings into the past was that the precursor of our Club was originally situated half a mile away in Fortis Green, East Finchley, and that the original course – of which not a trace remains today – has long since been the victim of the developers' hunger for building land.

There is one peculiarity about Highgate Golf Club that has made the reconstruction of its history more than a little tricky: the propensity to conflagration.

The clubhouse has burnt to the ground not once but twice over the years, and on both occasions the Club's records helped fuel the flames. So, for the author, finding out the facts has been as troublesome as discovering weapons of mass destruction in Iraq.

Nevertheless, it has been an illuminating and worthwhile exercise. I hope that you take pleasure in this journey into our precious Club's past.

Tony Hackett

Home ground: a view of the 18th hole looking pretty – and pretty unplayable – in snow.

1 ANOTHER TIME, ANOTHER PLACE

According to a notice that used to be displayed above the bar, Highgate Golf Club was founded in January 1904. But that does not tell the whole story. The 1904/1905 edition of *The Golfer's Annual* refers to the "Highgate and East Finchley Golf Club" – instituted in January 1904. It was only in 1906 that "East Finchley" was dropped from the Club's title. And thereby hangs the first tale in our intriguing history.

The East Finchley Golf Club was born in October 1893 at Fortis Green – as the crow (or a straight drive) flies less than half a mile from the present course. The land was leased from the Church Commissioners. The East Finchley Golf Club is shrouded in mystery as few records have been traced, and few members of Highgate will even have heard of the club.

The files at the Church of England Record Office reveal that, in the autumn of 1893, "certain Gentlemen" approached a farmer called Lane, who ran a dairy farm at Fortis Green under a lease from the Church Commissioners. The "Gentlemen" asked Farmer Lane if they could use part of the land for the purpose of playing golf. Lane agreed that they could use a limited area for golf during the winter months of 1893/94.

James Willington Lane was born in 1825 and his Manor Farm was sited near the now defunct playing fields adjoining the 7th fairway. It was quite an enterprise: when Lane died in 1903, a local newspaper reported that there were 70 employees at his funeral.

The earliest letter on the Church Commissioners' file concerning our particular golfing heritage is dated 7

Long gone: Manor Farm, home to James Lane's thriving dairy business.

August 1894 and is from the land agent, Cluttons, who acted for the Commissioners. The letter refers to the fact that the tenant (Farmer Lane) had granted permission to "some gentlemen" to play golf on some of the leased fields. These people had formed themselves into a club called The East Finchley Golf Club and wanted to put the arrangement on a more permanent basis. Cluttons suggested that a seven-year lease be offered to 12 responsible members of the Club in respect of 38 acres at a rent of £100 for the first year and £125 per annum for the remaining six years.

In view of what happened later, it is interesting that a condition was imposed that "the Lessees give up the whole of any part of the land at any time during the term upon the receipt of one month's notice to quit in the event of the land being required for building, road-making or other purposes".

The Commissioners retained the right to fence any footpaths running across the land. No golf was to be played on Sundays. These conditions were acceptable to the members apparently, for the Commissioners instructed Cluttons to agree to the proposition and draw up a lease, the terms of which were set out in a letter dated 30 November 1894. Twelve

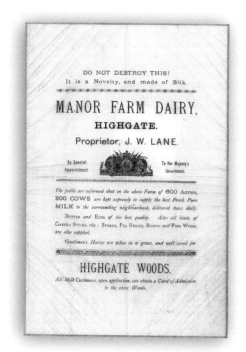

Flyer: Mr Lane's promotional material.

At the first AGM, the Treasurer reported a credit balance on the Club's accounts of £2.7s.10d, but there were outstanding accounts of £20 – no doubt members not paying up on time.

Eleven months into the life of the Club, the President was Walter Hill and there were 12 Vice Presidents: Messrs J.H. Hall, W.F. Sayer, S.F. Moginie, W.D. Perrott, J.J. Langdon, T. Newman, H.G. Stacey, J. McDonald, N.F. Harrison, the Rev. H.N. Collier and Doctors Hicks and Greenwood.

The Captain was Dr Wylie and the Vice Captain W.H. Pickard. There was a council of 13 members, and the elected auditors were Mr C. Munro and Mr C.W. Pearce. The Treasurer was Robert Mitchell and the Club professional was William Duncan.

By 1896, the President was still Mr W. Hill, but the Captain was now Mr G. Elliott and the Vice Captain Mr J. McDonald. The constitution of the Club had apparently changed – there was now a committee (not a council) comprising Messrs W.H. Pickard, A.E. Law, C. Hood, C.W. Pearce, J. Elder, J.J. Thomson and Dr Hicks. The Hon. Secretary and Treasurer were Mr J.W.P. Scott of 17 North Road, Highgate, and Mr W. Minto of 41 Leicester Road, East Finchley. Duncan was still the pro.

Soon after the inception of the

members were named as representatives of the Club – the first name was a Mr Walter Neill of The Firs, East Finchley, whose occupation was given as an Advertising Contractor.

And so it came to pass that a nine-hole course was laid out and a clubhouse built. The club quickly prospered. Starting with just 18 members, by the time of the first Annual Meeting in September 1894, 110 men and 30 ladies had joined. The entrance fee for men was one guinea (£1.05 in today's money), and, for the ladies, half that sum. Annual subscriptions were three guineas and one guinea respectively.

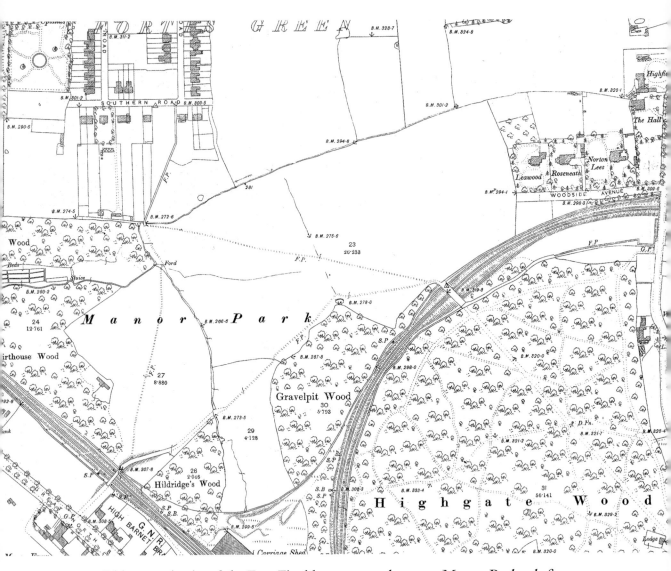

Old ways: the site of the East Finchley course – shown as Manor Park – before the builders moved in.

Club, the committee approached the local MP, Mr H.C. Stephens, to see if he would agree to be the first President. The September 1894 AGM was told that he had replied that "he believed the Club was a grand thing for Finchley" and he "would have accepted the position as President but did not understand the game".

"Golf is evidently a very popular pastime in the neighbourhoods of Muswell Hill and East Finchley", reported *The Hornsey and Finsbury Park Journal* on 15 September 1894, covering the story that 300 people turned up to see Duncan, the pro, play a match against the Muswell Hill pro, called Gow.

The paper reported that "the weather on the whole was not altogether unfavourable, for notwithstanding the keen, cold winds, and the at times threatening clouds, the sun shone with unwonted brightness during the whole of the time the competition was in progress. After capital play by both men, Duncan, who was in excellent form, won by eight and six".

It must be presumed that although the course had only been in existence for a short time, it was of a reasonable standard for this match to have been played.

One of the first Vice Presidents of the Club, Mr J. McDonald, and Mr

George Elliott, a council member and subsequent Captain, both came from, and had a close association with, the town of Luton in Bedfordshire. The nearby South Bedfordshire Club had started in 1892, and, as a result of the connection, the East Finchley Club participated in a match to commemorate the opening of the new South Beds GC clubhouse in the autumn of 1895. As a consequence, a series of matches, home and away, took place regularly until at least 1906. The South Bedfordshire Club has kindly allowed us to quote from its history.

The first recorded inter-club match was played on 12 October 1895 against East Finchley and was a special match held to commemorate the opening of the new pavilion (at Luton). South Beds won the match by 37 holes to nil – the report stresses that the East Finchley team was not at full strength. East Finchley were considered to be one of the strongest teams in the south, and South Beds enjoyed a long series of matches against them. The results of the later matches confirmed that East Finchley were missing some of their better players for the first encounter.

The first match was described in the article covering the opening of the Luton clubhouse, and the Dickensian style supports the belief that the reporter was determined to take over the mantle of the great man, who had died only 25 years earlier,

Due to the chalky sub-soil which made for fast greens, the home team won as a result of their putting, the reporter claimed, but he went on to say:

"In more than one case the Finchley men were distinctly superior to the opponents in driving, some of the latter being, like Jehu, furious drivers. The opening drive of the match was over a hedge about 12 feet high and some 50 yards away, and nearly everybody succeeded in getting over successfully. There were one or two who 'funked' and went round".

Although tea was provided immediately after the match, the main celebrations were held over dinner at the George Hotel. During the drive to Luton, "a splendid idea was hatched that the golfers should wear red coats to wit. And this was done".

During the speeches that followed the meal, Mr McDonald, the East Finchley Vice Captain and an old Lutonian with long-standing associations with the South Beds Club, offered to provide a trophy to the value of £20 to be played for by South Beds members.

Mr Law of East Finchley offered a handsome knife as a prize for the best individual score during the match between the clubs. Unfortunately, Mr Law won his own prize, but later gave another to be awarded with the McDonald Trophy.

The return match against East Finchley was played on Saturday 7 May 1896, and on this occasion the East Finchley team took ample revenge for their earlier defeat. The home team won by a massive 102 holes to 2 in a 14-a-side match. The press cutting report on the match gives a vivid impression of the day's entertainment, and one could be forgiven for believing that it was as a result of these early matches against East Finchley that the expression "social match" was first coined.

The team left Luton on the 9.05 train and arrived at Finchley at 10.30. After being greeted by the Vice Captain, Mr McDonald, the teams played a friendly foursomes just to familiarise the Luton team with the course. At one o'clock the entire Luton party of 22 was driven to Colt Hall, Fortis Green, the home of the East Finchley Captain, Mr Elliot, where they were entertained to lunch.

The match proper commenced at 2.30, with the last returns being made at 6.30. Hugh Cumberland was the only winner on the Luton side, and four players, Mr Giles, Mr F. Simpson, Mr T. Ottoway and Mr E. Greatorex, were beaten by 11, 12, 12 and 14 holes respectively.

Following the game, the two teams and their supporters adjourned to the Midland Grand Hotel for dinner and an evening of convivial entertainment. Speeches and toasts were only interrupted when members of the party stood to entertain the gathering with songs that included – 'Goufing', 'The Gay Tomtit', 'The Bandoliero' and 'The Zuyder Zee'. The party returned to Luton on the midnight express.

Matches against East Finchley continued for many years, and although the London side generally proved to be the stronger, the atmosphere surrounding the matches was always that of an important social occasion rather than a hard-fought golf match. The atmosphere of these matches was probably best captured in a later report which described how, following dinner and a convivial evening at the George Hotel, the South Beds hosts accompanied their London guests to the station and hailed their departure by rendering 'Will Ye No Come Back Again' from the platform as the train pulled out.

Because of the connection, the East Finchley professional, William Duncan, played in the first professional match at the South Beds Club on 16 September 1896 against the Carnoustie professional Alex Smith.

Matches between the two clubs were still being played in 1905, when a drawn match took place on June 17 at Highgate, where the East Finchley Club had moved the previous year – changing its name in the process to the Highgate and East Finchley Golf Club.

The South Beds Club had its Centenary in 1992 and kindly invited Highgate to participate in a match as part of the celebrations.

By 1896, the Secretary of the East Finchley Club was Mr I.W.P. Scott. On 4 February 1896, he wrote on behalf of the committee to the Church Commissioners, requesting a reduction in the rent (this became a regular request in later years). The bone of contention concerned the public right of way across the course. The local council, Hornsey District, was insisting "that a public right of way exists through the centre of the ground... ", threatening the Club with legal proceedings if they played across the paths. According to the Secretary, this had: "a very detrimental effect on the position and welfare of the Club, as it prevents their making use of a considerable portion of their ground and so restricts the number of members the Club had hoped to find room for, thus giving them a smaller revenue than they had every reason to anticipate."

The letter continues: "The free use

made by the public... of such footpaths is a source of much annoyance and inconvenience and has already prevented several gentlemen, who would otherwise have done so, from joining the Club ".

The letter went on to say that, because of the sodden state of the ground in the winter months, the Club was having to make a much larger outlay for drainage "than was ever anticipated". For these reasons, it was felt justified to request a reduction of the rent, which had only been agreed two years earlier at £125 per annum. This was referred to Cluttons, who suggested that, in the circumstances, it was not an unreasonable request and the annual rent was duly reduced to £100.

By January 1898, the Secretary of the Club was Mr A.W. Pearce, and he wrote a letter to the Commissioners on another sore point with the members: "Now that Sunday play is becoming so very general whether there would be any objection to the withdrawal of the restriction inserted against Sunday play in the lease." He went on to remind them that "...the Club pays a heavy rental, has spent a large sum of money amounting to several hundreds of pounds in draining and improving the course and erecting a golf house and protecting the land from encroachment by the public, but the committee find it a difficult matter to

retain sufficient membership to recoup them for their outlay unless the Club can offer the same facilities other clubs enjoy".

It was hoped that: "the question of Sunday play would receive favourable consideration... play on Sundays would cease at one o'clock and no caddies would be employed". To support this request, it was mentioned that the active membership included "the Vicar of Muswell Hill, the Curate of All Saints, Caledonian Road, the Minister of the Congregational Church, East Finchley, Churchwardens and Sidesmen of St. James Muswell Hill, Deacons and Officers of the Nonconformist Churches in the neighbourhood, members of the District council, local medical men and a number of gentlemen representing the professions etc. All these people... would esteem it an inestimable boon to have the opportunity of a game on Sunday mornings particularly during the winter months". The impassioned plea was turned down flat by the Commissioners.

In later years, Highgate Golf Club engaged the Commissioners on the same subjects (rent level, Sunday play and encroachment on the land). The clerical landlords did not relax their ban on Sabbath golf until the thirties.

By the end of the 19th century, the

Report of the Hospital Committee.

The Report No. 9 of the Hospital Committee was then brought up, as follows :—

REPORT OF THE HOSPITAL COMMITTEE.

No. 9.

1.—**Supply of Milk, &c., to Hospital.**—The Committee considered the referred letters received from Mr. C. H. Crees and Mr. J. W. Lane, Joint Managing Director of the Manor Farm Dairy, Limited, in regard to the Contract for the supply of Milk, Butter and Eggs to the Isolation Hospital, Mr. Crees applying for the consent of the Council to the transfer of the Contract entered into by him to the Manor Farm Dairy, and Mr. Lane undertaking to supply Milk, &c., of satisfactory quality. The Committee recommend that the Manor Farm Dairy be allowed to continue the supply for the present at the prices mentioned in the Contract

4.—**Trees, Middle Lane and the Topsfield Estate.**—The Committee had before them letters received from Messrs. I. Edmondson and Son, of No. 8, The Broadway, Highbury Park, N., in regard to the planting of trees in Middle Lane and on the Topsfield Estate. The Committee recommend that consent be given to the planting of trees in Middle Lane only, the roads on the Topsfield Estate being not more than 40 feet wide respectively.

5.—**Footpath from Fortis Green to Highgate Woods.**—The Committee had before them a letter received from Mr. F. Nicholls, of "Lyndhurst," Fortis Green Road, requesting the Council to put in force the powers vested in them to prevent the obstruction of the public footpath leading from Fortis Green to the Highgate Woods, it being rendered dangerous to pedestrians by the game of Golf being continually played across it at several points by Members of the East Finchley Golf Club. The Committee gave instructions for inquiry to be made.

6.—**Highgate Hill Tramway.**—The Committee had before them a letter received from the Parliamentary Agent of the London County Council, proposing the insertion of a clause for the protection of the District Council in the Bill which the County Council are promoting in Parliament for obtaining power to work certain Tramways, including the Highgate Hill Tramway. The Committee gave instructions to the Solicitor to the Council to agree to the insertion of the clause referred to.

50

10th June, 1895.

Mr. J. J. Langdon, a member of the Council, was read, stating that Mr. George Elliott, who had proposed to meet the Committee, was unable to attend, and mentioning, on behalf of the Club, that arrangements would be made during the following week for the alteration of the "teeing" grounds and course so as to obviate the necessity of playing across the public footpath. It appeared, however, that there were more public footpaths than one affected, and accordingly the Clerk was instructed to write to the Honorary Secretary to the Club and intimate that the course must be altered so that the members would not play across either of the public footpaths which are at present interfered with.

large increase in the number of houses in the District, it is necessary to provide altogether six additional dust carts at an early date, and they accordingly recommend that prices be obtained from three or four leading firms, and that two carts be purchased at once, and four others after September next.

8.—**Bakehouses.**—The Committee had before them the referred matter of the inspection of bakehouses in the District, which is having the attention of the Medical Officer.

9.—**Public Footpaths near Highgate Woods.**—The Committee further considered the application in regard to the obstruction of public footpaths by the playing of the game of golf by members of the East Finchley Golf Club. The Honorary Secretary to the Club was communicated with, and notice given to him of the meeting of the Committee, in case members of the Club desired an interview with the Committee. A letter received from

10.—**Sewer Ventilator, Fortis Green.**—The Committee have had before them letters received from Mr. William Armitage, of "Westerlee," Fortis Green, in regard to a sewer ventilator near to his house on the Fortis Green Road, and, after viewing, recommend that the position of the ventilator be altered and its height increased.

11.—**Storm Water Culvert, Barrington Road.**—The Committee, after viewing, recommend that the storm water culvert from Barrington Road through the Public Pleasure Grounds be now completed.

12.—**Public Footpaths Near Highgate Woods.**—The Committee viewed the fields near the Highgate Woods which are occupied by the East Finchley Golf Club, and consider that these fields are quite unsuitable for the playing of the game of Golf, on account of their being to so great an extent intersected with public footpaths that the continuance of the playing of the game is a source of danger, and accordingly recommend that the Club be so informed, and requested in the interests of the public safety to discontinue playing.

Don't fence me in: Hornsey council minutes of 1895 recorded the comings and goings over footpaths on the East Finchley course. Top: Dealings with Mr Lane's dairy.

Strange moves at Muswell Hill

At that time, our neighbours at Muswell Hill Golf Club had been threatened by their landlords (the Ecclesiastical Commissioners again) with the loss of part of their course, an action that would have prevented them continuing with 18 holes on that site.

The Muswell Hill members then made arrangements to continue their club at a new site, and had obtained the land that is now the home of the South Herts Golf Club at Totteridge. But the Church Commissioners changed their minds, and the Muswell Hill Club found itself with its existing 18-hole course plus the land for a second 18-hole course at Totteridge. In the event, the South Herts Golf Club became established in its own right, with some of the Muswell Hill members joining both clubs. A number of the shortly-to-be-homeless East Finchley members moved to the Totteridge club, and it is recorded that some of them attended the South Herts GC annual dinner in 1904.

East Finchley Club had become well established, part of the great golf boom of the eighties and nineties. It has been calculated that only 20 or so golf clubs existed in England before 1879, yet by the 1890s a new golf club was being formed every fortnight, and, by the end of the century, there were 500 golf clubs in England.

The growth of golf during this period was matched by another sort of expansion. The development of London, already rapid, gained further momentum and the pressure on landowners to use, or sell, their land for building was intense. The Church Commissioners were not immune to this trend – and it was almost inevitable that they would wish to sell the land at Fortis Green for housing.

The nearby town of Muswell Hill was expanding rapidly and many of the houses that spread from its centre date from the last two decades of the 19th century. It cannot, therefore, have surprised the golf club committee when their landlords advised them that they were desirous of lapsing the leasing arrangement once they had obtained the necessary planning permission. The local newspaper reported an application before Sir Cory Wright, the chief

Hornsey magistrate, and permission was granted for the land to be built over subject to certain restrictions concerning the rights of way across the land – the paths that had caused the East Finchley golfers such aggravation over the years. The result was that the landowners agreed to incorporate pavements, which would, in fact, provide more public access than was previously the case.

It cannot have been a great surprise to the East Finchley Club committee when its landlords advised that they wished to lapse the lease.

The fate of the East Finchley Golf Club was sealed and the membership had to decide how and where they were to continue to play their beloved game. Members seeking a local alternative were heartened when

the Commissioners offered them a lease on farmland adjoining Bishop's Wood and Kenwood, then the seat of the Earl of Mansfield. A lease was drawn up with eight individuals acting for, and signing on behalf of, the new Club.

So it was that, in 1904, the East Finchley Golf Club vanished forever from Fortis Green, reborn as the Highgate and East Finchley Golf Club on the land on which we display our golfing skills, or otherwise, to this day.

On the following five pages, you will find Ordnance Survey maps published between 1873 and 1996, showing the amazing growth in development of what had previously been a rural area to the north of the capital.

The Professionals at Fortis Green

William Duncan* 1894-1896

B. Skuse* 1896-1897

William Winton 1897-1900 (a founder member of the PGA in 1901)

J. Webb 1900-1902

A. Tooley 1902-1904

* Duncan and Skuse are both listed in contemporary golf publications as being greenkeepers, but that was a common description for a professional before 1900.

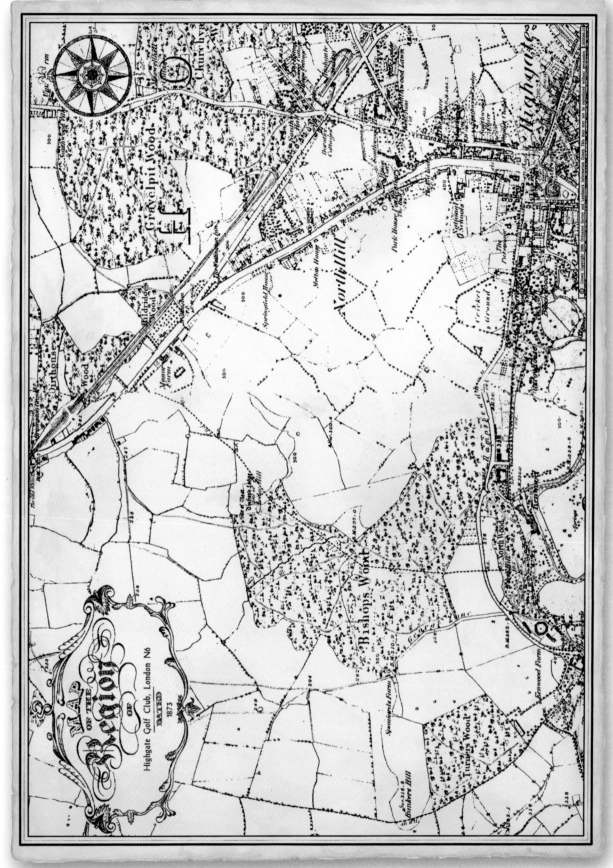

MAP *OF THE* **Region** *OR* Highgate Golf Club, London N6 **DATED** 1873

1873

MAP OF THE Region OF

Highgate Golf Club, London N6

1896

TRACED

1896

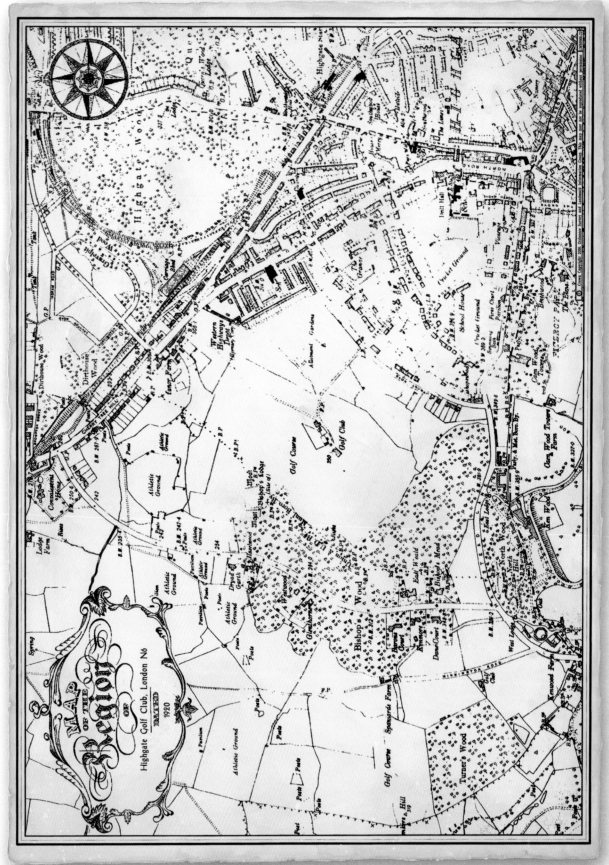

MAP OF THE **Region** OR

Highgate Golf Club, London N6

1920

1920

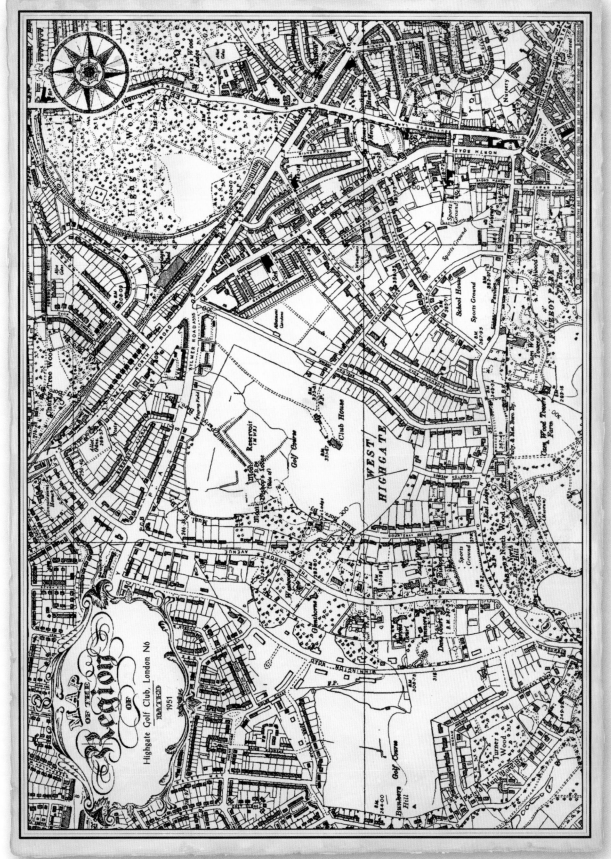

MAP OF THE Region OR Highgate Golf Club, London N6

1951

WEST HIGHGATE

1951

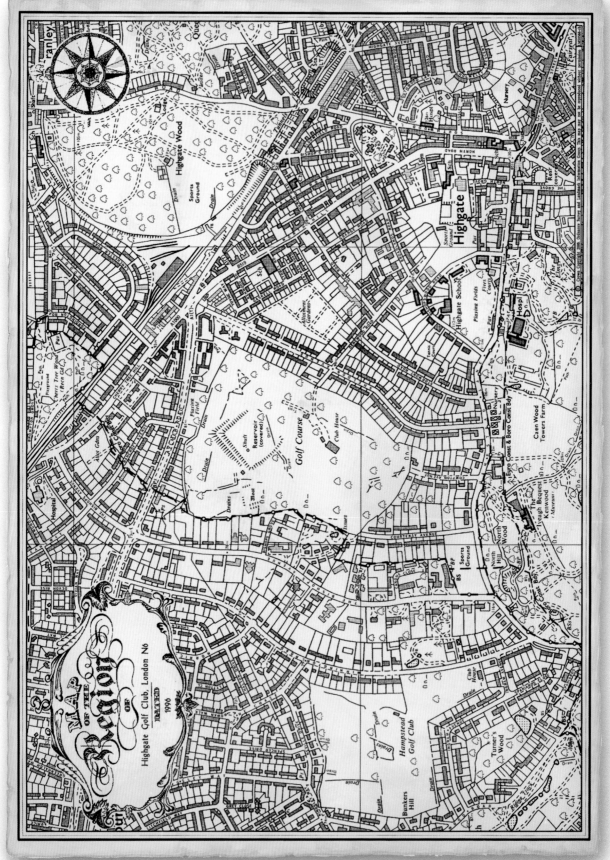

MAP OF THE REGION OR Highgate Golf Club, London N6
TRACED 1990

1996

2 *THE LAND*

One of the first reactions to the news that golfers were on the move to a new home next to the Bishops Wood was protest – from cricketers.

Certain cricket clubs had, for some time, been permitted to play cricket on the level parts of the land to be leased by the Church Commissioners to the golfers evicted from the East Finchley site. It is not entirely clear who had previously encouraged the cricketers – Farmer Lane, the tenant, or the Commissioners themselves. A hastily-arranged protest meeting was called as soon as the plans for the new golf club became public knowledge. Following this meeting, a certain Reverend Llewelwyn H. Parsons wrote to the Commissioners, in a letter dated 16 January 1904, complaining about the proposed loss of the land to cricketers, but his objections fell on stony ground. The cricketers were offered alternative sites in the area, but it is not known whether the offer was ever taken up.

In February 1904, a draft lease was drawn up and agreed by five individuals, the lead name being a Mr James John Thomson of "Baveno", Broadlands Road, Highgate. The term offered was for 14 years at a rental of £318 per annum in respect of an area of 79 acres and 2 roods. The lease also allowed for lawn

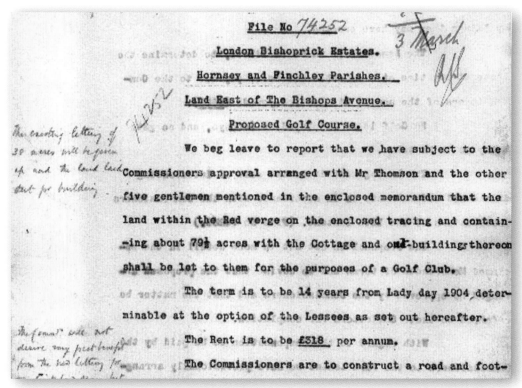

Right lines: the first page of correspondence regarding the original club lease.

tennis, which was very popular at that time, and bowls to be played, but there is no evidence that these activities ever took place. The lease did not permit play on Sundays or the sale of "intoxicating liquor" to non-members, except on two occasions a year when the permission of magistrates had to be obtained. The actual lease was dated January 1905.

Golf Illustrated magazine of 26 February 1904 reported as follows:

> A new club, to be called the Highgate and East Finchley Golf Club, has been formed to acquire a lease of 80 acres of very suitable land for an 18-hole course adjoining the Bishops Wood at Highgate. W.M. Winton, the well-known Acton professional, and authority on inland greens, is laying out the course, and is of the opinion that the land is eminently suitable for the purpose, the turf being of excellent quality and the formation of the land, which is of an undulating character, lending itself to natural drainage.
>
> The course, which is very

Breaking news: the club's arrival gets a mention in the Hampstead and Highgate Express.

picturesque, will be of a sporting character, and an excellent test of golf, several of the holes exceeding 400 yards, and crossing has been entirely avoided.

A commodious clubhouse is to be erected on the highest part of the links, affording a very fine view.

There will be access to the links from Highgate, from the Great North Road and from Bishop's Avenue.

Although the clubhouse can be reached in about half an hour from King's Cross, the course has all the attractions of a links many miles from town, and is strictly private and secluded.

The list of members is rapidly filling and the present entrance fee is likely

to be shortly increased.

The work of draining and laying out the course has already made great progress and Winton hopes to have the links open for play early in the summer. The Honorary Secretary is J.H. Moritz of West Bank, Broadlands Road, Highgate.

In 1905, the entrance fee was four guineas and the annual subscription the same, but, the following year, the amount extracted on joining had increased, as forecast, to six guineas. Between 1905 and 1906, the number of members increased from 360 to 470.

It is difficult to establish exactly when play started on the new course, but the local newspaper reported, on 18 February 1905, the results of the Medal competition (gross 89 – handicap 8 – net 81). The magazine *Golf Illustrated* reported in April 1905 the results of the final competition at Fortis Green: a ladies' bogey event on 28 March won by a Miss R.C. Blakelock, then the Lady Captain.

The new club was clearly going from strength to strength. The *Illustrated Sports and Dramatic News* of 27 July 1907 had pictures of the Ladies' Section Summer Meeting.

The Highgate Golf Club brochure, published in 1927, mentions that the course was "laid out by Billy Winton,

THE ILLUSTRATED SPORTING AND DRAMATIC NEWS.

JULY 27, 1907.

930

The Sportswoman.

An engagement is announced interesting to lady golfers, being that of the Yorkshire lady champion, Miss R. Gascoigne Moeller, to Mr. H. Harrison, the only son of the late Mr. Harrison, of Ilkley, who has been for many years a partner in William Williams Brown and Co.'s bank, Leeds.

Miss Moeller was not present at the open meeting held by the Harrogate Club at Starbeck, which was most successful. Mrs. Houghton, from Huddersfield, won the first prize with 106—22—84, Mrs. Constant (Scarborough) being next with 103—18—85.

The July medals played for at Ganton resulted in a win in the first class for Mrs. Haworth with 88—16—72, and Mrs. Bell (30) with 70 net in the second class. The ladies' foursomes for July were won by Miss Whitehead and Miss D. Hanbury, and Miss Anderson's prize by Mrs. Wilkinson with the fine return of 93—29—64. The Ganton ladies journeyed to Headingley to play an inter-club match, which they won by three matches to two. A match between Leeds and Huddersfield at Cobble Hall was won easily by Leeds, Huddersfield only scoring one point. Teams of nine a-side from Rotherham and Wath met on the Thrybergh links, the former club winning by three points. Fifteen monthly competitions have been played for the President's Bowl at Wath, and eight ladies qualified for the final, in which Miss E. S. Wigfield and Miss F. J. Stanley tied for first place with 63—12—51. On the replayed tie Miss Stanley won, making a record for the course of nine holes with 59. The summer meeting of the Cleveland Club was held at Redcar, in which Mrs. Jervis, at York, won the putting event with 42.

A match took place on the Whitley course between the club and South Shields, the local team winning every match. West Lancashire and West Derby met at the latter club but in this case the visitors won easily in singles and foursomes. The fifth qualifying round for the Captain's Prize at West Derby resulted in a win for Mrs. Fitzgerald and Mrs. Manigold with 104—14—90.

Mrs. Holloway put in better scores, but had qualified previously.

Mixed foursomes were played at New Brighton, and Mrs. Johnson and Mr. Boote came in the winners with 6 strokes in hand. Miss E. Terry, with 114—25—89, won the medal at Hesketh, where Miss E. Crook and Miss M. Massey tied for second place. Miss N. Graham, who is a frequent winner at Hoylake, won the July medal with 87—9—78. Miss Wall, who was second, returned 84, the lowest gross score.

In the south the Brighton and Hove Club had a good turn-out for their medal, which was won by Miss Wainwright (28) with the good net return of 66. Mrs. Gerald Moor took the scratch prize and first class medal with 84—8—76.

The Essex County Golf Association held a successful meeting at Romford. The prize given by Mrs. Leopold de Rothschild was won by Mrs. Nicholls with 100—18—82, Miss Du Cane being next with 89—6—83, and Mrs. Cuming third with 85 scratch. Miss Glanfield won the driving prize, and Miss Richardson the putting prize after a tie with Mrs. Read.

The result of the county matches to date is interesting. In the north Yorkshire and Cheshire tied in points and in individual wins, and a match in a neutral green will be played to decide. In the Midlands, Staffordshire leads with 10 points and 30 individual wins, but has played four matches to Worcestershire's three, that county at present scoring 10 points and 27 wins. In the south-west, Gloucester is leading with 4 points and 18 wins, but has played three matches, whereas Devon has scored 4 points and 12 wins, with one match played. In the south-east, Sussex is again leading, having won 14 points and 44 wins in nine matches, while Surrey has scored 14 points and 43 wins in ten matches. Each club lost three matches, but Sussex scored by a walk-over. The Queen was at Sandown on Friday, looking so handsome and interested in the racing, and so merry and bright. She wore a charming dress of white and

Mrs. Fitzgerald, second medal winner. *Miss Hall, captain of the club and a "plus 4" member.* *Miss Wallace, the medal winner.*

THE HIGHGATE LADIES' GOLF CLUB SUMMER MEETING.

Dressed to thrill: the ladies' section Summer Meeting of 1907 was reported in the Illustrated Sports and Dramatic News. *In the background of the top photograph, haymaking is in progress near what is now the 7th fairway.*

who, at that time, was the professional to the (now defunct) Acton Golf Club". Winton was no stranger to north London, having been the East Finchley pro from 1897 to 1900.

However, the curriculum vitae of Cuthbert S. Butchart, a golf pro and course designer, refers to the fact that he "remodelled" the Highgate course in the period 1904/05. It is possible he acted as an adviser to Winton. Butchart ended his career in the USA but only after an unwelcome stay in Germany. At the outbreak of war in 1914 he was, unfortunately for him, in Berlin, designing a course, and was interned by the German authorities for two years.

HISTORY BENEATH THE 12th

Now happily ensconced in the new golfing home, and oblivious to the high drama that was to unfold over the coming years at Highgate Golf Club, members with a taste for history could look back over the centuries and discover some interesting facts about their patch.

More than 1,000 years ago, the land on which the course lies was thickly wooded and known as Hornesey (later Hornsey) Park. It is thought William the Conqueror hunted wild boar in the area.

Norden in his *Speculum Britannica*, published in 1593, refers to:

"...a hill or fort in Hornesey Park and so called Lodge Hill, for that thereon for some time stood a lodge, when the park was replenished with deare, but it seemeth, by the foundation, it was rather a castle than a lodge... It did belong to the Bishop of London."

The park around the Lodge Hill edifice was extensive, covering most of the land to the west and north of what is now Hampstead Lane. Lodge Hill is marked on maps as the site of the Bishop of London's hunting lodge, complete with moat. Historians estimate the lodge was built in Norman times; the Bishop acquired the building in 1293.

An early Victorian surveyor calculated that the building measured about 70 yards square. This suggests it was more than a lodge and was probably a substantial fortified building. In 1593, it was described as "old and overgrown with 100-year trees growing on the foundations".

It is over 500 years since the last Bishop resided there, and over time the building fell into disuse and disrepair. It is said the tower of the old Hornsey Church (the remains of which can be seen in Tottenham Lane) was constructed from the stones removed from the lodge when it was finally levelled. The spring that supplied the moat with water was filled in and now drains into the nearby Bishop's Avenue.

Evidence of the building itself can no longer be seen, but the remains of the moat and earthworks are still visible as golfers climb up to the 12th green. The local Archaeological Society approached the Club in 1982, asking for permission to carry out a dig, but, after consideration, the request was refused by the Club.

It is thought that Robert the Bruce, who was to become King of Scotland, stayed at Lodge Hill in the year 1305, and, being in great danger, was warned to flee. The

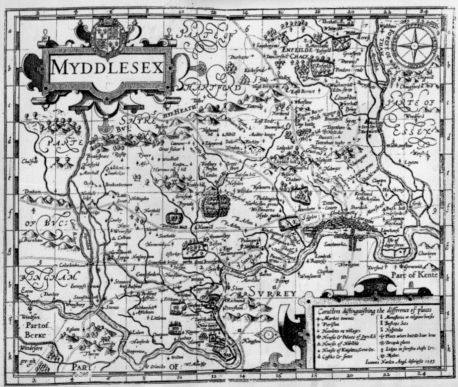

Lodged in the past: extracts from Norden's Speculum Britannica, *1593, referring to the ruins of the Bishop's lodge.*

Under the 12th green: artist Amanda Attenburrow's impression of the Bishop's lost lodge.

warning was in the form of a spur with a feather attached, and this is now incorporated in the crest of the Club.

A local tradition, which contradicts this story, is that the Bruce took refuge in a woodman's cot located on what is now Southwood Lane in Highgate. On that spot, centuries later (1879), a large house called Southwood Court was built by a Mr S.J. Johnson. Legend has it that it was one of Johnson's forebears who took the spur to Robert the Bruce, who awarded the crest to the Johnson

Wings of hope: the club crest.

family in gratitude. During the construction of Southwood Court, a stone was placed on the main chimney showing the family's crest – the winged spur. When the house was demolished in the 1960s, the stone was removed and cemented into the wall in Southwood Lane where it can still be seen today.

The Church Commissioners had, for many years, leased the land where the course is now situated to the Lane family, and when the land was leased to the golfers, the family continued to farm on the remaining land at Manor Farm. This disappeared in the 1930s when the new Aylmer Road was built across

Hard evidence: the chimney stone from Southwood Court, now to be found in Southwood Lane.

the farm. So farming continued to be squeezed out of London.

A STRANGE WATER FEATURE

The underground reservoir is an unusual feature of the Highgate course. Henry Cotton, who was an honorary member of the Club, is alleged to have said that, in his view, the 9th hole, which climbs about 40 feet up and over the top of the reservoir, is the worst golf hole in Europe.

Since the end of the 19th century, and the rapid expansion of the population of London, the Metropolitan Water Board had sought sites for reservoirs in order to provide ever-increasing amounts of water to an unquenchable capital. In north London, part of the Highgate golf course was one of the sites selected (there were others in Highgate Village and in Dartmouth Park Hill).

The first mention of the proposed reservoir is in a letter from the Club dated 29 September 1924, addressed to the Secretary of the Ecclesiastical Commissioners on the subject of the Club being granted a longer lease. Passing reference is made as follows: "The site of the new reservoir is provisionally arranged within the

Hole lot of trouble: the Metropolitan Water Board had no plans to cover the concrete.

boundary of the Links, but the position of the Golf Club and its playing rights over the same are fully covered…" In a letter from the Ecclesiastical Commissioners' agents, Cluttons, dated 20 November 1924, we find the following: "…that the construction of the reservoir may be postponed but will be required at no distant date". Unfortunately for the Club, it was not long delayed and it was built in 1928/29.

As mere leaseholders, the Club did not appear to have been involved in any discussions with the Metropolitan Water Board and presumably had to accept a fait accompli.

During the period of construction, the Club lost a number of holes, and once building was finished, the layout of the course had to be changed to take into account the new topographical feature. The 16th hole on the original course became the present 9th hole, for instance.

Noises off: the racket from the construction machinery put golfers off their stroke.

HGC member Ian Wallace recounts that, when the construction work was completed, the Metropolitan Water Board left the concrete top of the reservoir bare, but his father, then MP for Dunfermline, and other committee members, complained to the chairman of the Water Board, who agreed to put down a layer of earth and to grass over the whole structure. As Ian Wallace commented: "At least we still have 18 holes, which would not have been the case without some very tough negotiating by the committee, led by my father".

There have been problems over the years with leaks from the reservoir, and, in 1999, new drains were laid at the bottom of the bank in front of the 10th green. In 1975, the Water Board reported signs of pollution and instructed that no chemicals were to be used that could leach into the stored water.

Wall of water: the coming of the reservoir was a dark day for Highgate Golf Club.

Sometimes the reservoir was put to imaginative use by members. Rodney Wilkinson and his father used the bank as butts for pistol target practice. They both had Luger pistols and shot at old tins (presumably not on competition days). Also in years gone by, when snow was a more regular winter feature, a number of members would use the sides of the reservoir as a short ski run.

In February 1932, the then secretary, Col. A.C. Soutten, wrote to the Ecclesiastical Commissioners: "The Club is suffering from a very special handicap in that a very considerable portion of the Golf Course... has been sold... and a reservoir constructed on it. The seriousness of this change was unfortunately not realised until the construction began, but the course has been so seriously injured... (it was affecting membership recruitment.)

View from above: to the left of the reservoir construction site can be seen the present 9th and 15th greens (then the 16th and 13th).

Although the Club now plays over the recently completed reservoir, it is found that the assertions that the ground would not be injured are completely falsified by the event, and that the ground over and about the reservoir is waterlogged and extremely unsatisfactory and unattractive."

GROWING PAINS

In 1918, the Club received income of

£200 on the sale of hay, but the 1920 accounts reveal that this source of income fell away. In fact, costs were incurred restoring that part of the course "under hay" and also in removing the allotments set up to produce vegetables during the Great War. The 1920 accounts also reveal that "4 new Greens have been made". Total expenditure increased from £2,349 to £4,064 and income from £2,349 to £3,134 – hence a loss, and an increase in the subscription for

Getting the measure of the 9th hole

HIGHGATE GOLF CLUB
STANDARD SCRATCH SCORE 69

Player _____ Date _____

Competition _____ Handicap _____

Strokes Received _____

Marker's Score	Hole	Yards	Par	Stroke Index	Player's Score	Won Lost Halves +−O	Marker's Score	Hole	Yards	Par	Stroke Index	Player's Score	Won Lost Halves +−O
	1	285	4	13				10	355	4	14		
	2	320	4	9				11	195	3	8		
	3	370	4	3				12	275	4	16		
	4	120	3	17				13	370	4	10		
	5	335	4	11				14	375	4	6		
	6	460	4	1				15	440	4	2		
	7	520	5	7				16	470	4	4		
	8	150	3	15				17	160	3	18		
	9	480	5	5				18	325	4	12		
OUT		3040	36				IN		2965	34			
							OUT		3040	36			
							TOTAL		6005	70			

Marker's Signature _____

Player's Signature _____

Handicap ...
Net Score ...
Bogey Result ...
Par Result ...

Strokes are to be taken at those Holes opposite which the red figure is equal to or less than the total Handicap Allowance.
In bogey play the score must be entered otherwise the hole will be counted as lost.
Unlabelled alterations on score cards in Stroke Competitions shall disqualify the player and unlabelled alterations in Bogey Competitions shall disqualify the player for the hole at which the breach of this Rule occurs.

	COMPETITION			TIME		Please indicate which tee used.

DATE _____ COMPUTER NO. _____ H'caps _____ Strokes Rec'd _____

PAR 69 SSS 69 □ PAR 69 SSS 67 □ PAR 71 SSS 69 □ PAR 71 SSS 71 □

Player A _____

Player B _____

Hole	Marker's Score	White Yards	Par	Yellow Yards	Stroke Index	Score A	Score B	W=+ L=− H=0 Points	Red Yards	Par	Stroke Index
1		296	4	272	13				284	4	13
2		322	4	308	9				305	4	9
3		384	4	352	5				349	4	3
4		117	3	106	17				113	3	17
5		337	4	321	11				322	4	11
6		462	4	439	1				407	4	1
7		521	5	500	7				472	5	7
8		154	3	134	15				123	3	15
9		440	4	437	3				403	5	5
OUT		3033	35	2868					2778	36	

PLEASE AVOID SLOW PLAY AT ALL TIMES

Hole	Marker's Score	White Yards	Par	Yellow Yards	Stroke Index	Score A	Score B	Points	Red Yards	Par	Stroke Index
10		366	4	346	14				333	4	14
11		197	3	187	8				164	3	8
12		278	4	266	16				240	4	16
13		351	4	336	4				306	4	6
14		376	4	350	10				346	4	4
15		443	4	417	2				415	5	10
16		470	4	456	6				416	4	2
17		151	3	126	18				110	3	18
18		320	4	320	12				308	4	12
IN		2952	34	2804					2638	35	
OUT		3033	35	2868					2778	36	
TOTAL		5985	69	5672					5416	71	

Stableford Points or Par Result _____

HANDICAP _____ NETT _____

Holes won _____ Holes lost _____ Result _____

Marker's signature _____ Player's signature _____

The making of a monster: cards of the course before (above) and after (left) the re-classification of the 9th hole. Note the alterations to the stroke index.

After the construction of the reservoir was completed, the 9th hole was shown on the card as having a length of 480 yards – a par 5. In the seventies, a zealous member, Tom Crompton, measured the hole and discovered that it was actually 451 yards – below the minimum for a par 5. The par was reduced to 4, and, as a result, it is now one of the more difficult holes on the course.

men members from £4.4.0. to £5.5.0.

The 1920 annual report mentions that the loss would have been £102 greater had it not been for the generosity of certain members who had bought a motor mower for the Club. Some pictures and a sideboard had also been presented.

One of the main reasons for the rocketing expenditure was the increase in wages on the course from £450 the previous year to £1,153. In 1920, the total membership was 615, with 306 full male and 124 lady members and the balance being made up by other categories.

HANGING ON

The original terms of tenure granted to the Club by the Ecclesiastical Commissioners were for a 14-year lease at an annual rent of £318 per annum. As mentioned before, various conditions were imposed. The most onerous from a golfing viewpoint was that no play was allowed on Sundays and restrictions were applied to the sale of liquor.

In March 1913, the Club committee approached the Commissioners about extending the lease after 1918. With only five years of the original lease to run, the Club was experiencing difficulty signing up new members. Agreement was reached to extend the lease for a further seven years from March 1918 at an increased rental of £353 per annum.

In the summer of 1916, at a time when the battles on the Somme were about to commence with huge loss of life, the committee approached Cluttons, the agents acting for the Commissioners, to point out the adverse effect the war was having on the Club's finances and requesting a reduction in the annual rent. This was duly considered and it was agreed to reduce the rent payment by £90 for the 18-month period to March 1917. The Commissioners wished to encourage the Club – its presence helped in the sale of the surrounding land for house building. Also they were aware that a "large part of the Course is now being used for vegetable growing…" – the Club was helping the war effort at a time when German submarines were sinking a large number of merchant ships bringing food to Britain.

In June 1919, the committee again approached the Commissioners requesting a further extension of the lease, pleading (again) that, as the lease term was so short, it was a hindrance to the Club in obtaining new members. The committee was clearly very persuasive: a further extension was agreed for another seven years (to 1932) at an increased rent of £351 per annum.

In June 1924, the then President, Percy Hurd, and the Captain, Frank Runchman, requested a meeting with the Secretary of the Ecclesiastical Commissioners, and they met on 25 June to discuss a long-term lease extension.

This approach by the Club was successful and the Commissioners agreed to offer a new 21-year lease from 1925. The rent was set at £400 until 1932, when it was due to increase to £450 per annum until 1946. One condition was that the Club should "...regularly cut the thistles and at all times keep cut and levelled the mole and ant hills." Still no play was permitted on Sundays.

However, on the sale in 1928 of 27 acres to the Metropolitan Water Board for the development of the underground reservoir, the rent was reduced for the remaining acres to £260 until 1932 when it increased to £298 per annum.

At the beginning of 1935, the Club again approached the landlords, requesting a further lease extension. A 32-year lease was offered at a rental of £800 a year. The club haggled and beat the landlords down to £600 for five years and £800 for the remaining years. This took the Club's tenure to 1967.

It wasn't long after the outbreak of the Second World War that the Club started feeling the effect of hostilities. Early in 1940, it was reported that membership had fallen by about one-third; green fees had dropped by a similar amount. The club anticipated a loss of about £1,300 by the year end and the rent was about to increase to £800. In view of the financial state of the Club, a reduction was requested, and, as a result, the rent was reduced to £400 for the year to March 1941.

By the midsummer of 1942, the Club approached the Church Commissioners in the light of a loss of £800 for the previous 12 months to March 1942. At a meeting with the freeholders, it was revealed that since the war started, the membership had reduced from 500 to 360 and expenditure had been reduced by 60% with the number of men employed dropping from 13 to 3. It was agreed to continue with the reduction to £400, for which the Club was very grateful.

In early 1955, the Club again approached the Church Commissioners to negotiate a new and extended lease. A new lease was offered for 33 years to run to 1988 at an annual rental of £900. The securing of the longest lease yet reflected the concern of the Club committees over security of tenure.

A NEW LANDLORD?

A report appeared in the *Daily Telegraph* of 22 January 1935, claiming that Hornsey Council was negotiating with the Church Commissioners with the aim of purchasing the freehold of the land on which Highgate Golf Club stands. It appears that the Club was also interested in acquiring the freehold, but felt it had insufficient resources for this purpose. The Club had, in fact, been in discussions with Hornsey Council over a period of years, hoping that, if the Council did purchase the freehold, it would lease the land back to the Club for 25 or even 50 years.

The Council wanted to be able to guarantee that the land would not be built on, and would remain an open space. Somewhat ominously, however, it was mentioned in Council meetings that, in the future, the value of the land would undoubtedly increase substantially if used for building purposes.

Sometime in 1932, the Ecclesiastical Commissioners had indicated verbally to the Council that they would accept £34,000 for the freehold of the 52 acres (the course area minus that portion sold to the Water Board for the reservoir site). In October 1934, the Club was formally offered the freehold for £37,500.

The Hornsey Council minutes dated 21 January 1935 are of interest:

"There is only one undeveloped area of any size left in the Borough of Hornsey – The Highgate Golf Course – and for many years conversations have been proceeding between representatives of the Town Council and the Highgate Golf Club with the view of ascertaining whether a scheme could be devised whereby, without incurring any loss to the rates, the Council could assist the Club to acquire the freehold and so secure this area from building. At the present time the Club are in possession of the greater part of the area, at a low rent, under a lease from the Ecclesiastical Commissioners, which has some twelve years to run.

"In May 1933 your committee requested the Mayor and Town Clerk to discuss with the representatives of the Golf Club a scheme which is apparently favoured by the Minister of Health and has recently been adopted with success in the neighbouring districts of Wood Green and Friern Barnet.

"This scheme consists in the purchase of the Freehold by the Local Authority and the leasing of the land to the Golf Club by the Local Authority at a rent equal to the loan payments – i.e. a rent which will just ensure that no loss will fall on the ratepayers.

"Negotiations with the Freeholders [the Ecclesiastical Commissioners] were opened up by the Club but your committee regret to report that no progress has apparently been made, except that the Club have ascertained the price at which the EC would be prepared to sell.

"The matter is complicated by the fact that in the event of the Club's succeeding in obtaining this freehold they would also require to secure on reasonable terms a renewal of their present lease from the Water Board, who own a portion of the golf course, but so far as your committee can judge, this should not be too difficult to arrange.

"In these circumstances your committee recommend that the County Council should be informed of the facts, and that the Council should confirm the offer which has been made to the Golf Club, tentatively, by this committee.

"In submitting their recommendation, the committee are obliged to point out, in order that the Council may be aquainted with all the facts, that the development of the golf course by building, on town planning lines, would not result in a pecuniary loss to the Borough. They are, in fact, advised that development would result in a considerable pecuniary gain to the ratepayers, after making provision for all the public services required in connection with the new houses."

This minute is interesting in that the original intention of the Council was stated to be to ensure the course remained an open space, yet refers to the possibility of building on the land.

For whatever reason, the purchase was not pursued further by the Council or, for that matter, by the Club. After the Second World War, the Borough of Hornsey was absorbed into what became Haringey Council. The history of the Club might have been very different had they become our landlords.

TO HAVE AND TO HOLD

As mentioned above, in 1934 Highgate Golf Club had been offered the freehold of the land remaining in the possession of the Ecclesiastical Commissioners (the course area apart from the portion sold to the Water Board for the reservoir) for £37,500.

We now move forward to 1957. In that year, the Church Commissioners had been made aware by their professional advisers of the provisions of the Town and Country Planning Act 1954, under which it was possible to obtain compensation in the event of planning permission being refused.

The local press reported in October 1957 that Hampstead Golf Club, which had purchased its freehold from the Church Commissioners in 1930, were to be compensated to the extent of £70,857 under the provisions of the Act and this concentrated everyone's minds. It also unleashed much controversy locally with one local councillor referring to it as "legalised robbery" (presumably of taxpayers).

Harold Bedales OBE was an eminent member of Highgate Golf Club, a solicitor who was the Town Clerk of Hornsey Council – and also the Hon. Solicitor to the Club. In 1958, Bedales assisted in finding out whether compensation could be obtained under the Act. He also established the concession from the

landlords that the Club, with a 30-year lease to run, would be entitled to part of any compensation.

The discussions continued into 1959, and, in view of the complicated legal situation, the Club and Church Commissioners jointly obtained counsel's opinion and acted on it. After further detailed negotiations, it was agreed:

- Any compensation would be split 50/50

- The Church Commissioners would sell the freehold to the Club for 20 times the annual rental.

The Club agreed to this on the condition that compensation was obtained.

The annual rent was then £900, which meant the club could buy the land for £18,000 – a considerable reduction on the price demanded in 1934.

The Church Commissioners duly made an application for planning permission to develop the course and this was (as expected) turned down. As a consequence, compensation was paid under the Act amounting to £31,248. Under the agreement with the Church Commissioners, the Club received half of this, amounting to £15,624. This meant that the Club

HIGHGATE GOLF CLUB

DENEWOOD ROAD, N.6

22nd August, 1960

Dear Sir (or Madam),

The Committee have pleasure in informing you that, in accordance with authority given at the Extraordinary General Meeting held last year, the freehold of that part of the Course (52 acres) held on lease from the Church Commissioners has been acquired by the Club. The purchase includes the Golf Club Buildings.

As the land has been zoned as an open space and cannot be built upon, a substantial sum by way of compensation has been claimed and received from Government sources, with the result that the actual cost to the Club of buying this freehold was no more than £2,286, which has been found out of the Club's resources.

The purchase will save a rent of £900 per annum, but some tax will be payable. It also eliminates the necessity to provide for dilapidations (freeing the investments held by the Club for this purpose) and abolishes the former Landlord's restrictions.

Apart from Stamp Duty and Registration Charges no legal or other costs were incurred by the Club in connection with the purchase.

After several years of delicate negotiations the transaction has now been completed and the Committee thought it proper that the Members of the Club should be informed.

The Committee are most grateful to the Church Commissioners for their help and cooperation.

Yours sincerely,

F. J. FERGUSON,
Captain.

NOTE.—The Club remain Lessees of the land (28 acres) owned by the Metropolitan Water Board but the Lease has been extended and now has 29 years to run.

Smart move: the Captain's letter to members regarding the freehold purchase.

had to raise only £2,376 to reach the purchase price. In effect, the Club bought the freehold of the land for this figure plus costs.

This was no doubt considered to be a very satisfactory arrangement. Much credit was due to Harold Bedales for masterminding the whole matter.

After the purchase of the larger portion of the land, this still left the 31 acres leased to the Club by the Water Board. The Club became part freeholders and part leaseholders, and that situation continues to this day.

The lease period on the land owned by the Water Board (and then its successor, Thames Water) had always been for a much shorter period than had been the case with the Church Commissioners and it is apparent, again from correspondence, that, over the years, the committee was often concerned about the lack of security of tenure. For instance, in the early 1980s, a refurbishment of the interior of the clubhouse was put on hold until a new lease period had been agreed with the Water Board. At the back of the committee's mind must have been the possibility that the lease would not be renewed, or that the Club would not be able to afford the terms requested. With hindsight, this does not appear to have been a problem, the committee possibly being over-prudent in its concern.

A potentially more dangerous matter was the possible effect of the Community Land Act of 1975. Reference has already been made to the possibility, in the 1930s, of the then local council, Hornsey, purchasing the freehold to ensure the land remained an open space. It has already been mentioned that, in one council debate, it was recorded that one councillor averred that if ever planning permission was obtained, the value of the land would be considerably enhanced to the benefit of rate payers.

One of the provisions of the 1975 Act was thought to be that when the lease of land owned by a public body, such as the Metropolitan Water Board, fell due, the local authority in whose area the land was situated would be enabled to purchase the freehold, or take on the lease. The Water Board land stretched from Aylmer Road, across the derelict land to the right of the 7th fairway, part of the 7th fairway and all the area of the reservoir. If this area had been leased to another party, it would have had a seriously adverse effect on the Club, especially if the land was then used for non-golf purposes. Following the

The threat that built up

Express & News, June 14, 1974

'Homes on the fairways'

POVERTY GROUP'S PLAN TO BUILD ON GOLF COURSES

HARINGEY Council was told this week —"You have the land—get on and build new homes."

Haringey's Poverty Action Group said in their first housing bulletin that the council had land and should build in Highgate, Muswell Hill, part of Crouch End playing fields, golf courses and Alexandra Park race-course.

The bulletin rejects the council's claim that no more land is available for building and says that councillors are afraid to act because of "the powerful lobby whose self-interest would be threatened."

"Families living in bad conditions are less likely to be re-housed now by the council than they were two years ago," say the group, who outline a plan for finding land for building.

It is a plan which must cause an uproar in Highgate and Muswell Hill.

For the group recommend buying by compulsory purchase orders and demolishing houses with large gardens in this area, to increase the housing density to the same proportion as Tottenham.

"There are over twice as many rooms per acre in Tottenham as at Haringey's western end. We suggest that housing densities of up to 100 rooms per acre should be allowed throughout Haringey."

The group also want Haringey Council to redevelop the two private golf courses at Highgate and Muswell Hill.

"They are a luxury Haringey can't afford and should

be redeveloped, partly for housing, partly for public open space. By this means alone half the families on the waiting list could be rehoused."

Councillor George Meehan, chairman of Haringey's housing committee, had reservations about the group's proposals.

"I agree that it would be a good idea to increase the housing density in the western part of the borough and we are slowly buying up property as it becomes available," said Mr Meehan.

"But compulsory purchase orders on large houses in Highgate and Muswell Hill would be much too expensive. And I know that there is a long lease on Muswell Hill golf course, though I would like the courses to be open to the public. We have been trying to buy Crouch End playing fields for the past two years, but there, too, I would prefer to see it developed as a leisure facility rather than used for building.

"Environmental aspects are very important for the future and I think the answer is for more land to be made available by other boroughs."

● Well, if you're going to have a crash, what better place to choose than outside the offices of an insurance expert!

Yet only one person was injured — Mr Thomas Shepherd, driver of a Bedford lorry, who suffered cuts to his back from flying glass. He received treatment at New End Hospital.

Four vehicles were involved in this accident on Rosslyn Hill, Hampstead, last Friday afternoon.

Mr Shepherd's lorry was in collision with a Morris 1000 car and then a parked delivery van, which in turn collided with a stationary post office van.

MARTHA'S WINE BAR

A potential threat to the club was revealed in 1974, with reports of views by some councillors in support of a compulsory purchase order with a view to building council flats on the 5th and 6th fairways and to turn the rest of the course into a 9-hole municipal course.

It is a moot point whether planning permission would have been obtained, particularly bearing in mind Hornsey Council had, 40 years earlier, wished to maintain the land as an open space, but luckily, this never had to be tested. The newspaper article that appears here gives a flavour of this threat to the continued existence of the Club (and also the Muswell Hill Golf Club).

A field too far

In January 1990, the land owned by Thames Water to the right of the 7th fairway was being used as a playing field for schoolchildren. The owners were undecided what to do with the land, and offered it to the club on a two-year rental at £4,000 per annum.

The committee decided this was not of interest.

reorganisation of local councils at that time, this area fell within the boundary of the Borough of Haringey, and some of the actions of that council, as a potential landlord, led to apprehension amongst the committee and members.

But the danger, if there ever was one, passed.

THE CLUB AT WAR

In 1938, with war clouds looming

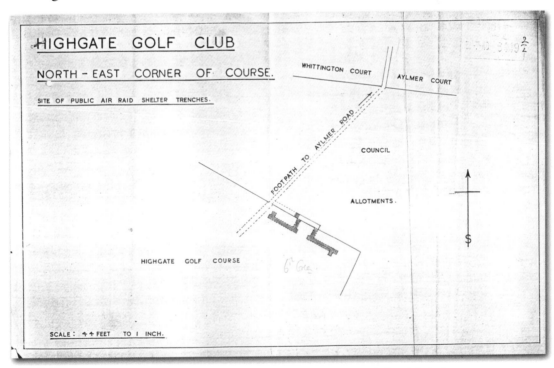

Take cover: the plan of the air raid shelter near the green of the 6th hole.

Shot hole: the World War Two barrage balloon, tethered in the car park.

over Europe, correspondence took place between the Club and Hornsey Borough Council concerning the provision of air raid shelters for the protection of the population.

Eventually the council built a shelter with the capacity to accommodate 100 people on Club land near the 6th green. The entrance was via an opening in the adjoining allotments.

Apart from golfers who happened to be on that part of the course during a raid, one wonders for whom the shelter was intended. Correspondence shows that the intention was to provide for anyone

within half a mile who would otherwise have been in the open during a raid.

A little later, correspondence took place concerning the siting of a barrage balloon which, with its associated hut, was eventually rigged up on the car park. Material for the Norwegian Air Force was also stored on the car park.

When war was declared in 1939, the committee decided to suspend entrance fees, discontinue competitions and to give special facilities for play to members of the armed forces. The committee also introduced what they termed "drastic economies"; for instance, during the winter months, the men's lounge was closed throughout the week in order to save on heat and light costs.

During the war, part of the course was taken over for food production and this land was not returned to the Club until the early 1950s. Betty Whipple, who joined the Club in the 1930s and was twice the Ladies' Captain, remembers "digging for victory" on the members' allotments on the 5th hole. The 7th fairway was also used for food production.

Members played or practised so long as they had balls, which were in very short supply during the war. The loss of five holes to the war effort meant that a shortened course had to be devised. Some holes were played twice to produce an 18-hole round. The greens were kept in a reasonable condition, apparently.

The wartime Club Secretary was Col. A.C. Soutten MC, organiser of the local Home Guard. The course came within the region of responsibility of the 7th Battalion of the Middlesex Regiment Home Guard, who patrolled the course. One of their duties was to apprehend any German parachutists who might attempt to invade Highgate. As far as is known, none were observed and certainly none captured.

Bombs, mainly incendiary ones, fell on the course during the war, as they did on the neighbouring Hampstead course. In one raid, a high-explosive bomb penetrated the 18th green but luckily failed to explode. The bomb disposal squad appeared and, in digging down to retrieve the ordnance, did considerable damage to the green.

Rodney Wilkinson, whose father was Captain in the 1930s, remembers peering down the hole and seeing the bomb (which had at that stage presumably been defused). Rodney recollected that the green looked like a building site, with piles of earth everywhere. It is thought that, in total, more than 25 bombs were dropped on the course during the war.

The father of member Betty Gray, Ernest A. Mills, was Captain in 1941-2 and President in 1946. She comments that, during the war, there were numerous unexploded bombs on the course, which had to be avoided, and the odd landmine or two. Betty remembers her father playing most weekends during the war. His frequent partners were Sydney Taylor (Captain 1944-6), Guy Curtis (Captain 1948-9) and John Wilkinson (Captain 1954-5). The members of this high-status fourball were collectively known as the House of Lords.

When the Club Secretary's present office was constructed in the 1980s, builders digging the foundations discovered a bomb shelter. It is not known when this was built and whether it was constructed as a consequence of the bomb that had been embedded in the 18th green.

ENCROACHMENT

In the light of subsequent events, it is interesting that the first known case of encroachment was in February 1964 and concerned a property in Courtney Avenue. This situation was resolved satisfactorily, but, as a consequence, the greens committee was instructed to check all the boundaries.

The committee discussed further encroachment in March 1965 near the 8th tee, where fencing had been removed. Following investigation, the committee decided a modern two-wire fence should be erected on the boundary line, but there is no evidence that this was ever carried out.

In June 1974, the encroachment at the 8th was again noted and in January 1977 the matter was again discussed. By July 1979 the Hon. Solicitor had written to five householders along the 8th tee, but had received only two replies. The matter was pursued again in October. And so it went on.

The subject of this encroachment continued to be unresolved over the succeeding years. Eventually it was considered necessary to spend a considerable sum on a legal investigation and advice, and it was not until the late 1990s that an agreement was reached with a certain householder that the land encroached upon would be returned to the Club when the owner vacated the property.

Natural beauty: a watercolour by Norman Wilkinson showing a view up to the clubhouse in 1945, probably from the present 14th fairway.

British Golf Clubs : No. III.—Highgate

THE PAVILION (FRONT ELEVATION).

IT was down the famous Highgate Hill that the famous Richard Whittington came on his conquest of London, and a mighty Hill it is! I wonder if the Whittington story would ever have been written had the hill run upwards against the traveller, instead of making the approach to London from that side a sort of glorious ending to a long journey and an auspicious beginning to a great career!

Times have changed since Richard's time and so it is not a matter of great wonderment to find that the Highgate Golf Club, despite Highgate Hill! has a membership which overflows into a waiting list.

With tram cars running right up to the entrance of the Club at Manor Farm, Archway Road from the Highgate Station of the Charing Cross, Euston and Hampstead Tube and something just under a mile to walk if you take a ticket to Highgate Station on the Great Northern Railway, those whose democratic principles—in my case my principles are in this connection governed by absence of the requisite wealth!—do not permit of the possession of a motor car have not a very arduous task to reach the course.

And even if it were a matter of difficulty and not ease, it would be well worth while. It is a source of constant wonder to me to find how close to London one can get golf, and Highgate is another case in point. You step out of a bustling business area into the sweet cleanliness of a golf course and perhaps this sudden transition adds piquancy to the round.

At Highgate, you get a full size course with some thundering good holes, and none too easy. Mr. Blakey, the Honorary Treasurer and Secretary, is a wise man. He refused to indicate the best hole, and he argues that it is very much a matter of individual choice. That is to say that the man who does the long twelfth in bogey as a regular thing is quite persuaded that the eighth where equally regularly he drops a couple of strokes cannot be compared! And the man who does the eighth in par time after time and muffs his tee-shot at the twelfth every other round is not to be convinced that the twelfth is even a golfing hole! I have taken these two holes because they are in my opinion about the pick of the basket, although in saying this I don't want to seem to be decrying the other sixteen. The whole course is a very workmanlike job and the man who gets round in bogey has not got very much wrong with his game.

Highgate is a club which believes in the sociability of golf. It possesses a strong fixture list for the coming season and it is always good to find a club developing this side of the great game. It must be admitted that its accessibility has something to do with it : but the club is not always at home on its own course and there

The new Club Championship Shield. [[Golf Illustrated.

is nothing which improves a man's golf more or makes him a worthier golfer than playing on a variety of courses.

The club is developing all the time and the four new greens which were opened for play on the 19th May add to the value of the course. The surroundings are really delightful and the course reaches away down a slope from the club-house a little after the style of Hanger Hill. It is well bunkered artificially and every advantage has been taken of the lie of the land to make it a good test of golf.

The higher points on the course are said to give the finest panoramic view of Herts and Middlesex to be obtained round London, and they are at such an altitude that you are always sure of a breath of air and a moving breeze, however hot the day. This is a very real advantage as I found out for myself, for London was torrid the day I went to Highgate, and the golf course was almost as good a tonic as a breath of the sea.

The club house itself is not so elaborate as those possessed by certain other Metropolitan clubs : but it is by no means uncomfortable. The smoking room, which is illustrated, is a pleasant room, and the new club trophy—the Victory Challenge Shield—adds interest to the room.

There is one particularly attractive feature about the little year-book issued by the club. There is given the telephone number of each member possessing a private telephone—no small convenience this when you want a game in a hurry and have to try man after man before you find somebody as able and willing as yourself.

The Victory Shield, a photograph of which appears on this page, is a trophy of very artistic workmanship. In the oval frame at the top is a figure of Victory holding out a laurel wreath, for which a group of golfers can be seen employing their sternest effort. At the bottom of the shield are a soldier on guard and a sailor unfurling the Union Jack. Surrounding the two are the historic dates 1914 and 1919.

As we mentioned before, the club has a strong fixture list, and we give herewith a selection of the events which are due to take place during the rest of the year. They are as follows : Saturday, July 3—The Victory Challenge Shield, 36 holes, medal play, memento to winner. First round of 18 holes, Saturday, July 10 ; second round of the Victory Challenge Shield. Monday, August 2, Bank Holiday competitions. Saturday, September 25, the Elliott Challenge Cup, 36 holes, medal play, memento to winner, first round of 18 holes. Saturday, October 2, second round of the Elliott Challenge Cup. Tuesday, October 12, the Reid Challenge Cup, memento to winner. Monday, December 27, Bank Holiday competitions. The Ladies' Club has also a comprehensive list of forthcoming events.

Copyright]   A CORNER OF THE PAVILION LOUNGE.   [Golf Illustrated.

Copyright]   A GENERAL VIEW OF THE COURSE FROM THE 16th GREEN.   [Golf Illustrated.

Report: Golf Illustrated *carried a two-page profile of the Club in 1920. The lower picture above shows a view looking towards the present 14th hole.*

Changing with time: the 17th hole, pictured in the seventies.

3 *THE COURSE*

Mention has already been made concerning some of the consequences of the Great War, which started in August 1914. The main effect on the Club was the reduced number of golfers (and therefore subscription revenue) and the use of parts of the course for growing vegetables and grazing dairy cattle.

The following is one of the earliest impressions of the course, set down by an unidentified member remembering his childhood:

> The first sight, entering from Dene Road, was of large sheds containing what looked like farm machinery... and then you noticed the smell – the lovely smell of stables.

Both my father and mother were, I presume, founder members. I was born in 1906 and within four years I had two sisters and a brother. My mother never resumed playing golf, but her hickory shafted clubs were fully used by me in later years.

My main introduction to the course came about by the allocation of a plot of land on the course for members with families who wished to grow vegetables during the 1914-1918 war. Ours was carefully marked out in rough ground just forward and to the right of the then 4th tee [the present 5th tee]. Sheldon Avenue gardens adjoined. Deturfing had to be carried out in accordance with published advice, and care had to be taken to preserve the rolls of turf. We had to cope with horrible wireworms, double trench digging, wood ash fires, breaking up the large clods into smaller and then into plantable fineness. What we were to plant and grow, apart from potatoes, was still somewhat of a mystery but it all meant hard work and many prayers for fine weather.

Just before war was declared we had moved to Muswell Hill. We walked to the course through established allotments along a cinder path from the Manor Farm, gazing with envy at the simplicity of growing things. Our main attack with all hands was on Sundays when no golf was played.

There was great joy and excitement when something was sprouting through, but – horrors – could it be a weed? Yes, there were weeds but also a great profusion of vegetables, nice long lines just as the book said.

I used to watch the golfers keenly from our allotment. The vast stretches of greensward were lovely to gaze at... odd figures in the distance sometimes stopping to hit a ball – quite remote.

The fascination grew, and, at 10 or 11, I was wielding my own cut-down mashie – careful never to obstruct any real players.

This soon led to caddying for my father. Lessons on rules and etiquette were never to be forgotten, and in no time at all I became an expert tracker of the wildly hit ball.

In 1915 or 1916, the course was deprived of six holes, handed over to Manor Farm for its cattle. Competitions were also reduced – so many members were on war service.

For the sum of seven shillings and sixpence I became a schoolboy member, entitled to play on weekdays, but not on Saturday. The course was closed to everyone on Sunday – more hard work on the allotment beckoned. The clubhouse was regarded as quite a holy place, certainly not to be entered by children.

If rain prevented play, much of my time was spent in the pro's shed-cum-workshop. It was far more interesting for me to watch Fred Saunders skilfully shaping hickory shafts, fitting them to well-crafted wooden heads, then putting them on display at 12/6d. He also fitted steel heads to his own shafts, to sell at 7/6d.

I never had a lesson from the professional, being well instructed by my father: keep your head down; never hit out – you are not playing cricket now; keep your eye on the ball; replace all divots...

A cut above the rest

At the committee meeting on 12 December 1962, it was agreed that the 1938 grass cutter should be scrapped and replaced with a new Ransome mower at a cost of £89.

It was noted that, with the 1938 cutter, three men took a morning to cut six greens, whereas two men could cut nine greens in a morning with the new machine.

Before the proliferation of the internal combustion engine it was the practice to use gang mowers pulled by horses to cut the fairways. The Club produced some of the fodder and reference

has been made to the situation during the First World War, particularly the increase in the price of fodder. In the photograph on page 33 a horse-drawn gang mower can clearly be seen near what is now the 12th green. In the thirties, the Club changed from horse power to a petrol engine vehicle.

This vehicle was a "maid of all work", as described by Rodney Wilkinson (see his illustration). It was based on a flat-nosed 1928 Morris. It had no battery, just a magneto, and was started by swinging a handle. It had a dark green bonnet and box, black wings and grill, and red wheels. It was used all summer, towing a triple-cutting gang mower, and was for some years the only petrol-driven vehicle used on the course. The wooden box at the rear was used in the winter to distribute prepared soil for the greens. This was composed of fine soil, three-year-old leaf mould produced on the course, and sharp sand.

Fred Saunders [pictured on pages 111 and 115] never appeared outside his shed unless properly dressed: a Norfolk jacket, plus-fours. His son Clifford, a year older than myself, sometimes turned up during the holidays and was excellent company to play with. He had his own set of clubs – my father soon gave me my mother's set. These were made by Fred Saunders, and had not been used since my arrival. With only the replacement of the driver and the mashie, I played with those clubs until 1950. That small-headed brassie – ivory-faced – was sheer joy out of the rough. I was even told by a ruffled opponent that he was sure it was illegal.

I regret to recall that my expensive steel match set never gave me that same thrill as the hickory, with which I maintained a handicap of six – an excellent passport whenever I travelled where golf was played.

Apart from my father's tuition, I had the good fortune to meet a Scottish gentleman called Tait; I understood he was private secretary to the Earl of Dalhousie – the latter badly wounded in France and ensconced in a large house just behind the 17th green.

To me, Tait was absolutely the top of the tree. His handicap was said to be plus-six. He would appear about 4pm with just four iron clubs, all brightly polished as if with Bluebell. We would hurry to the 2nd tee – it was rapid golf from then on. He would quite frequently drive two off the tee if he thought the first was slightly out of line. He always spared time for my effort, and would now and then display trick shots, probably to entertain a young lady who occasionally accompanied him.

Being the proud owner of an Ingersoll Crown Pocket watch, I was absolutely horrified to see Tait place a gold Ingersoll face up on the tee, place a minim of sand on the face to hold the ball, then with a full swing hit the ball clear, pick up the undamaged watch and place it in his pocket. The obviously delighted female was said to be the Earl's sister. Tait rarely played more than half-a-dozen home holes, and never putted out.

Caddying for my father in the final stages of various competitions, I recall names of other senior golfers or low handicap players, most of whose names graced the club walls: Willie Don, Horace Holmes, Charles Beresford, Dr Anderson (false leg), the Lynne brothers (Hamleys Toys), Curtis (left-hander), Walker (the fastest swing I ever saw). I remember one of the aforementioned stated that he would be rather be playing a game called bridge... because it was raining.

I have recovered some silver spoons from a family home in Norfolk, one of which is a jam spoon inscribed "HGC Reid Cup Memento 1912. Attente Perfecte", along with a large spoon for the Lyle Cup and several which I think are monthly medal coffee spoons. There must be many more around with members' families. Winning a trophy was tough work, and in the final stages strict silence prevailed. It was permissible to clap

but only after the final putt had been holed.

I cannot be precise, but I would suggest that it was 1920 before some of the holes came back into play. They had been used for haymaking and much re-seeding and rolling was necessary.

To return to the war years, one happy and beneficial sight on a sunny Sunday (no play) was the arrival of a large open car packed with blue-clad mobile wounded soldiers. The car was driven by a tubby, peak-capped man called Peter Gallinni, said to be

A time of peace: wounded soldiers found the course an excellent aid to recovery.

the owner of a "pricey" West End restaurant. He was an Italian – then our allies. The soldiery disembarked to roam the course. Signor Gallinni presented exotic fruit and other food from the boot of his car to Mrs Hovel, wife of the head groundsman and catering manageress.

(Many hospitals and convalescent homes were set up in Highgate and Hampstead during the First World War, and the writer refers to the visits to the Club of wounded soldiers who received hospitality from members.)

Subsequent pages from this document are missing, but it gives a young person's view as to what the Club was like at that time.

COURSE LAYOUT

The layout as shown in the 1927 *Club Handbook* is basically the original from 1904 with certain minor alterations.

As mentioned in the previous chapter, during the construction of the reservoir at the end of the 1920s, the Club was forced to play over a restricted number of holes, with some holes being played twice in order to produce a full round of 18 holes. The major difference from the present layout is that the 1st green was on the site of the present 17th green and an extra hole was squeezed in so that the present 6th hole was the 7th on the original layout.

Once the reservoir was completed (1929) and the concrete top grassed over, a new layout was brought into play. This more or less retained the first 9 holes, but the 10th was the present 16th hole and the 11th the present 15th hole, after which a player would proceed down the present 10th as the 12th, the present 11th as the 13th and the present 12th as the 14th.

During the Second World War, the 7th and 9th fairways were ploughed for the growing of cereals, and this land was not released back to the Club until 1949/50. The course

A Norman Wilkinson watercolour showing a stack of baled straw on the 7th hole in 1945.

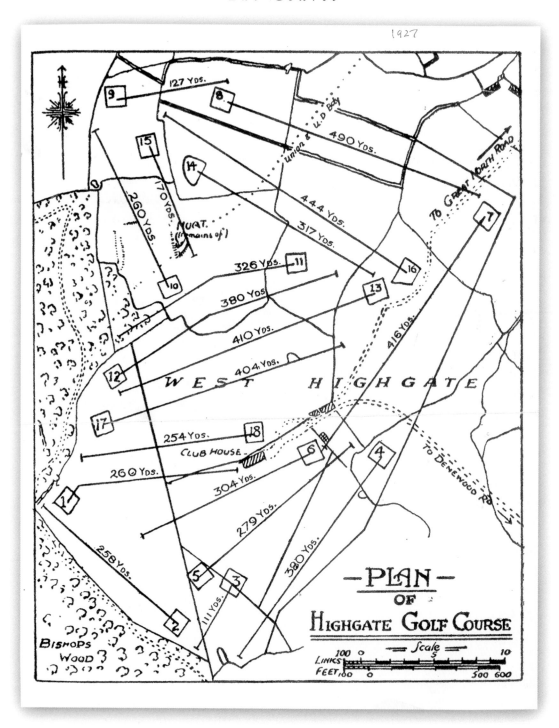

Altered course: the layout shown in the 1927 handbook had changed little since 1904.

Take your time: players putting on the old third green in 1921.

was consequently much shortened. The 7th fairway being out of play, the 7th hole was played from the present 7th tee to what is now the 9th green. The 12th was played from the area of the present 10th green to the present 7th green.

In the early 1950s, the course was again changed. The third green was moved from the present flat area at the bottom of the slope of the 3rd to its modern-day position. A new 4th hole was constructed – which remains in play today. The old 4th hole was played from a teeing area just to the left of the present 4th green to the present 3rd green.

The 5th tee was back in the corner of the course to the rear of the present practice area. This made the 5th a more challenging hole than the one we play today. However, too many households in Sheldon Avenue complained about the number of tee shots finishing in their gardens, so the tee had to be brought further

Shaping up: an aerial photograph of the course taken in 1949.

The way we were: the Club handbooks of 1965 and 1979.

New beginning: the new clubhouse under construction after the 1962 fire.

forward in order to reduce the risk. One of the Sheldon Avenue complainants, the then mayor of Hornsey, threatened the Club with an injunction at this time because of wayward drives landing in his garden.

The Club took a dim view of such a threat, especially as the mayor received the freedom of the Club during his term of office. It was perhaps not surprising that, at a later date, his application for membership was refused.

In a still later course alteration, the 8th green, which was then positioned to the right of its present site, had to be moved to the left and joined to the 11th green – wayward tee shots and, once again, the threat of legal action, were responsible for the move.

In September 1966, the course was re-measured, establishing an overall length of 6,005 yards. As a consequence, all handicaps were increased by one.

Over the years, the course has constantly been improved. For example, in 2001 major reconstructions of bunkers on the 11th and 17th greens were carried out, and in 2003 the 1st, 5th and 18th tees were rebuilt with the use of 60 tons of earth.

Later view: the course seen from the air in 1990. Drought conditions meant that old features, such as grassed-over bunkers and old boundaries, could be identified.

Taylor made: Sydney Taylor and chums made up a fourball nicknamed The House of Lords.

4 THE CHARACTERS

We start this chapter on some of the personalities that have made Highgate Golf Club come alive over the years with the story of the Titterton family, whose connections go right back to the very beginning.

The Rev. C.H. Titterton (1863-1958) was a founder member of the Club. He was the British Chaplain in Warsaw towards the end of the 19th century and returned to the UK around 1902. He took a house in the then fashionable suburb of Highbury Fields, where he had a living. His son, John C. Titterton, was born in 1906. John Titterton first played golf at Highgate in August 1914, when he was a junior at Highgate School. He was introduced to the game by his father, a keen golfer who had been brought up in Midlothian and had learnt his golf at Mussleburgh.

John occasionally caddied for his father, but mostly played with a schoolfriend. John believed that the pair were the first boys from the school to play on the course. His father, he said, "...liked the course other than the fact that it was situated on clay and the greens were very slow, particularly in the winter. There

The Titterton clan: founder member the Rev. C.H. Titterton (top right) with his family (top left). His son, John, is pictured above with his family shortly before his death.

were several mature oak trees and plenty of good old-fashioned rough. The various gradients made it a very sporting course." Sand was used for teeing purposes, and, even after wooden pegs appeared in the 1920s, many players continued to use sand.

John Titterton recounted to the author in November 1998 that in those early days, "I felt there was a great feeling of camaraderie in the club"; yet it was common practice then for members to address each other by using surnames only. His father was usually called "Padre".

The course was surrounded by woodland and farmland, and he remembers hearing gunfire as pheasants and other game were shot in the adjoining woods. His father was one of the early motorists and used to drive to the Club in his two-seater DeBion Bouton car. Those members who lived locally drove or walked to the Club, and those from farther away travelled by train to Highgate Station, where they would hire a taxi. Some came by bus via the Great North Road and would then walk to the Club along the path that ran through what are now the allotments behind the 7th tee and connected to the present path that runs from alongside the 15th green to the car park.

The Titterton family moved from Highbury to Croydon in 1916 in order to avoid the Zeppelin bombing raids, and John did not resume playing at Highgate until after the war ended in 1918, when the family returned to north London. John remembered that, up until the 1920s, the style of dress for men was woollen/tweed jackets worn with knickerbockers or slacks in the winter, replaced in summer by alpaca or linen jackets coupled with dark-grey flannel trousers. At all times, neckties were worn.

During the First World War, as well as parts of the course being used as allotments for vegetables, as described in the previous chapter, the rough was extended so as to produce fodder for the horse used to pull the gang mower. It was the practice during the war, with staff shortages as a result of the military call-up, for the members to help with course maintenance. John Titterton remembered during 1915/16 his father asking the professional, Fred Saunders, which greens needed cutting – the professional being in charge of course management in those days. He sometimes helped his father, acting as the "donkey" and hauling the heavy Ransome mower across the greens. Most members assisted with this chore.

Early days: a group of members outside the clubhouse in 1921. The Secretary,
Maclaughlin, is fourth from the left. Fred Saunders, the pro, is seated on the right.

The Secretary at this time was a man named Maclaughlin [pictured above]. John Titterton recalls:

"I well remember the arrival of Major Spain (Secretary 1921 to 1931). He struck me at the time as being a tall, heavily built man of a rather important demeanor. I never saw him on the course, but he was to be found playing bridge or in the clubhouse, or chatting in the bar. Although my usual golfing companion, Willie Buchanan, and I were fairly regular players at Highgate, I never remember either of us having a word with him. I think he may have disapproved of the "young entry".

Up until the end of the First World War, the membership tended to be of a "ripe age", but, after 1919, a new generation of golfers appeared, termed the "post-war brigade".

These included young men returning from active service, undergraduates, and other younger people.

Arthur Andress returns to Highgate after 80 years.

John Titterton played at Highgate from 1914 to 1924 and then again in 1929, after which he moved away from London. His father continued to play until the late 1930s. Latterly, John lived in Edinburgh and died early in 2000.

Arthur Andress (1900-2000)

Arthur was born in Highgate. His home was in Kenwood Road, off North Hill. He first caddied at the Club aged eight in 1908 and received three pence for carrying clubs for one round (adult caddies were paid 6d per round). If the member was playing 36 holes, a lunch, usually of corned beef and potatoes, would be provided in the caddies' wooden hut. The plate would have to be washed before being returned to the kitchen.

Arthur recollected caddying for a member called Mr Harvey, who lived at 1 Talbot Road. Harvey would pay him a farthing to clean his clubs – emery paper often being used for this purpose. A round normally took three-and-a-half hours, but there were some players who took much longer. A Club rule stated that, if players were being held up by those in front, the caddy should be sent forward and request that the following players should be called through. Arthur said the reaction of the players in front was not always a happy one!

Often, members would arrive at the Club in horse-drawn carriages, available for hire at Highgate station. If it was a competition day, the Club flag would be flown. Sand was used to tee up the ball when driving, and most members would have a hickory-shafted set of clubs comprising driver, brassie, niblick, two irons, mashie and putter. One ball used a lot at that time was the Dunlop 65, which he thought cost five shillings for four.

He thought the Club was very "strict" and, unlike Muswell Hill GC, would not allow an artisan section.

Arthur had various jobs, including working in Ballards Dairies in North Hill where he often started work at four in the morning. During the First World War, he volunteered for the army and joined a battalion of the Sussex Regiment. After training at Ripon in Yorkshire, he was sent to France and ended up in the Occupation Army in Germany until he was demobilised. He married in 1922 and never went back to being a caddy.

FIRE, BOMBS AND WATER

A reminiscence by **Ian Wallace OBE**

'For my entire life, my home has never been more than a mile away from the Club. For the past 30 years, it's been only a few hundred yards. As a child, I was aware that my father spent his weekends playing golf and that my mother played a little during the week. I'm pretty sure that in 1929 – when I was 10 – he was the captain. For a short time, his handicap was 8 and that gave him much pleasure. During the twenties he had to go for a short time to America on business. He sent us a postcard of the liner, the Mauretania.

I was disappointed. The largest liner then was the Majestic and I felt he should have been on that.

While he was away, his sister, my Auntie Chip, and her husband John, a Presbyterian minister from Derby, came to stay. One morning, a fire engine rushed along the road, its bell clanging. We all ran into the front garden. A great pall of black smoke could be seen rising over the rooves on the opposite side of the road. 'It's the golf club!' cried my mother, and she and Uncle John ran along Stormont Road towards the blaze.

I was firmly led back into the house by my aunt and Gwen, the parlourmaid (different days!), and allowed to go to the attic window where I could see little more than the smoke slowly diminishing in volume, and spent the rest of the morning imagining my mother and Uncle John burnt to death. In fact, they and other members managed to salvage some of the furniture, including a sofa. My mother was not tall but powerful.

The clubhouse was gutted, and I was allowed to go up and see the damage the next day. The sight I remember most vividly was scores of blackened iron clubheads. It was the era of hickory shafts. All the woods

70

A wonderful life: Ian Wallace OBE.

had gone completely.

The secretary at that time was Major Spain, a heavy-faced man who wore a monocle. It must have been the summertime because I remember he was wearing a fawn linen jacket. His lugubrious expression was like a St. Bernard dog that had lost its barrel. My mother sent a cable to my father in New York, telling him the news. By some error, the message he got was that our house had been gutted by fire. He had a bad few hours till the correction arrived.

Although I was only a child, I lived very much in an adult world. My father was in his early sixties at this time, and he and my mother, who was twenty years younger, talked freely in front of me and so I heard things that most kids would not have been privy to – including some alarming talk about how the fire had started. Though it was never proved, there was a considerable suspicion that arson was the cause. At that time, a city fraudster in the insurance world had been connected with a number of big and mysterious fires, and it was rumoured that he had been seen near the Club later that day. It was also rumoured that one of his assessors was at the scene almost ahead of the fire brigade. This comes under the heading of unreliable hearsay.

I don't think there were boy members then, and my only times on the course were on summer evenings when I was allowed to fly my Warnsford model aeroplane (hours of winding up the elastic) and tobogganing down the slopes in the odd hard winter.

During the 1920s, the Club suffered the tragic loss of part of the course to the Metropolitan Water Board. I think my father was either President or on the committee at the time. It became clear that the MWB were not going to grass over the concrete roof of the reservoir. My father and others fought hard and successfully to win back the lost holes. They may not be marvellous, but there they are. I'm proud of my father for many things and that's one of them.

Through those years, the pro was a delightful man called Fred Saunders. He had a good baritone voice, though his golf latterly was not really up to scratch or anywhere near it. When he retired, Tom Pierpoint, a tall, chunky young man with fair curly hair, succeeded him. He was a fine golfer and everyone liked him, but, when war broke out, he joined the RAF. It was a sickening blow when he was killed in action.

During the 1930s, both my parents were active Club members, both as golfers and bridge players. My mother was Captain shortly before the war and used to go off with a team of ladies to contest the Pearson Trophy. Another competition she often mentioned was The Harris Brown Bowl. I was away at Charterhouse and most of my holiday golf was played in Scotland, where we spent the month of August, or at Frinton-on-Sea in Essex, where we went at Easter. But I knew many of my father's Club friends. Names like Gilfillan, "Mac", Goodfellow (Chairman of Ever Ready), Lacey, Knox (whose son was the best player), Batchelor, Baker,

Wear, Grimes and Bedale (Town Clerk of Hornsey and brilliant Civil Defence organiser). I use surnames because I don't remember their first names. Surnames were the vogue at that time.

My mother went on to hold the captaincy throughout the war. The splendid Ladies Secretary was a Mrs Reid. Another stalwart was my mother's oldest friend, Anne Thomson. They organised working parties to make comforts for the troops and kept the ladies' side of the club going. All through her membership, my mother fought many battles to gain more recognition for the ladies, using a mixture of charm and robust argument. She wasn't an MP's wife for nothing.

When I was up at Cambridge, the year before the war I think, I was what was called a university member. One day in 1940, I played with my father, and, going down the 7th, we came upon an unexploded parachute landmine. It looked like a large Calor gas tank with a few knobs on. I went over to look at it and gave it a clang with my 3 iron. "Come away, you fool!" shouted my father, "It might go off." "They wouldn't let us here if it wasn't safe," I said with that maddening airiness of the young. He was right and I was wrong. About two hours later, the Army arrived and threw a cordon round it of several hundred yards while they bravely defused it.

The Secretary before and during the war was Colonel Soutten, a kindly man with a high, fluty voice which amused some of the members. He had won an MC in the First World War. I think it was at Christmas 1939, while I was still at Cambridge waiting to be called up, that he asked me to take part in a charity concert organised by the ARP (Air Raid Precautions) volunteers in a hall in Archway Road. His contribution was a revelation. He was a brilliant female impersonator and literally stopped the show.

Soon I was to lose touch with the Club for a long spell. I went into the Royal Artillery, but in 1942 contracted tuberculosis and was on my back for two years. I think I must have rejoined the Club in the very late 1940s. My musical and theatrical career took me away a great deal, and much of my golf was played in matches at other clubs for the Stage Golfing Society. I've always enjoyed my golf at Highgate, and members always seem to have understood that, in the theatre and musical world, you work at weekends. Indeed, once in mid-career when I turned up at lunchtime on a Saturday, one kindly member took me on one side and whispered: "Everything all right?" "Yes," I replied, puzzled. "Oh good. I thought perhaps the work had dried up, you being here on a Saturday."

I'll end this eccentric and episodic memoir in the middle of the night some time in the 1960s. The fire engines had forsaken bells for sirens, but they were pounding up Denewood Road to Highgate Golf Club's second fire. No aunt to stop me looking this time. Pat and I hurriedly dressed in the dark to avoid waking the children, alerted the mother's help and walked rather dazedly towards the gate. We were allowed no further. Standing there in pyjamas tucked into plus-four stockings, dressing gown, a homburg hat and smoking a pipe was the famous artist, Norman Wilkinson, who lived at the corner of Sheldon Avenue and Denewood Road. "Aren't you a little over dressed?" he said. In the light of the fire, I realised that, in the dark of the bedroom, I had hurriedly grabbed the striped trousers that went with my morning coat.

Soon there was a minor explosion from the heart of the fire and a sheet of white flame shot into the sky. "There," said a man with the rare experience of being an artist in two world wars, "goes a hell of a lot of gin."

John Bracewell

John is an old Cholmeleian who joined the Club as a junior in 1934. Here is his story:

'I was accepted as a full member in 1936 at the age of 14, with a handicap of 14. I remember the Secretary, Colonel Soutten. In those days, golf club secretaries were nearly always retired service officers, and Highgate was no exception. The thing I remember most about him is that, every Saturday morning at 9am, he used to stand at the entrance to the locker room and ask members if they were fixed. If they hadn't got a game, he would fix them up.

The professional was Fred Saunders, who was of short stature and then in his late sixties. He didn't aspire to win tournaments, but spent his time playing with members and giving lessons. I had a few lessons from him and my mother had dozens, being taught two or even three times a week.

It is interesting to note that, at Royal St. George's, one can see a Saunders aluminium putter in a glass show case. When Fred retired (in 1938), I remember seeing several pros who had applied for the job playing with the Captain and committee members.

In the end, they appointed Tom Pierpoint, a tall, fresh-faced young man with very light hair. He was a very good golfer. My father booked him every Sunday morning, and during the school holidays, I joined them. "Mac" Macmillan, who died in 1967, made up the four. Pierpoint never took more than 70 to go round, and, on one Sunday morning, I remember him going round in 63. I think he would have done well in tournaments, but sadly he was killed in the RAF in the war.

During the war, I allowed my membership to lapse, but rejoined in 1946. The pro was then Baverstock, and I gather he did not make a financial success of the shop. I remember the next pro, Fred Boobyer – he was a member of the well-known golfing family who did quite well in professional tournaments. Later, we had Laurie Ayton, the former Ryder Cup player from St. Andrews.

Among the other people I remember, pride of place must go to the already mentioned "Mac" Macmillan, who had the distinction of winning the Scratch Cup twice with an interval of 21 years (1912 and 1933). When I knew him, he played left-handed, but I do not know whether he was always left-handed or whether he had to change after the First World War, during

To the life: Tatler *captures the spirit of the Club in the year John Bracewell joined – 1934.*

which he lost a leg. In spite of having one false leg, he continued to play to single figures.

A prominent member in the thirties was A.V. Bridgeland (later Sir Aynsley Bridgeland), a very wealthy Australian tycoon who lived in Bishops Avenue. He died in 1966. He was a very keen golfer and played to low single figures, but he was a very wild hitter. Playing with my father in the thirties, he hit his tee shot at the 13th (now the 11th) into the hole on the 8th – a particularly amazing achievement as the 8th green was positioned well beyond its current location: the greens were not shared in those days.

On the subject of the 11th, I have happy memories of getting my first hole in one there with a 4 iron on 29 May 1949. To celebrate the event I stood on my head on the tee. On the two subsequent occasions I holed out, I also stood on my head, although with some difficulty in later years!

I used to have a regular game with Tony Haskins, whom I knew at school. It was unknown for us to put off a game because of the weather. On one occasion, we were playing in the monthly medal when the heavens opened and it sheeted down with rain. Tony and I carried on as usual, but everyone else on the course dashed to the clubhouse for cover. As we were the only players to complete the round and put in cards, I won the Senior Medal and Tony the Junior one!

The ceremony of the Horns of Highgate is very ancient and dates back to medieval times. I think Dr Bains introduced it as a competition to the Club. When I first remember it, the ceremony was performed by "Dickie" Gough, a master at Highgate School. I was asked to do it sometime in the fifties.

On one occasion, it was won by a Cholmeleian who was a friend of mine (possibly John Lancaster) so I decided to inject an additional piece into the ceremony and I poured beer on to the winners as they kissed the horns. This lark seemed to go down a treat, so I added it to the ceremony and continued it in future years. One year, this rebounded, as I won the horns and had beer poured on me by Bill Field (a master at Highgate School) who took over from me that year.

In the year of the second fire (1962) the Club's copy of the horns ceremony was destroyed. I found myself due to perform, but with no script. However, I remembered that there was a copy of the ceremony on the wall of the bar at the Wrestlers' pub in North Hill. The landlord lent me his copy and that year's ceremony was able to take place. **"**

Megan Evans

Megan joined in 1951 and remembers thinking the ambience then was rather like that of a country club. In the winter, there was always a coal fire in the lounge, which had window seats, sofas and standard lamps and was "very comfortable". She soon got to know other members by playing in the Wednesday morning competitions, which were usually followed by bridge in the afternoon. The Business Ladies played on Saturday afternoons. She remembers most men wore plus-fours. She recollects that the three-course lunch on Wednesday cost five shillings (25p) and the lunch on Sunday was so popular that there were regularly two sittings.

John Salisse

John Salisse joined the Club in 1956, when Norman Chamberlain was the Captain. John had been having lessons with Fred Boobyer, the professional, but was not acquainted with any members. The professional spoke to the Captain and John subsequently had an interview at the bar one Sunday morning, and was

duly elected a member. Life was much simpler in those times.

He was given a handicap and, although only a beginner, he found it easy to get a game at weekends by hanging around on the putting green. Usually the stake was a golf ball or sometimes a ball for each 9 holes and on the match overall. In those pre-breathalyser days, the custom was that everyone bought a round so, as most people played in fourballs on Sunday mornings, beer consumption particularly was maintained at a good level.

Sunday lunch in those days was very popular and usually there were two sittings. The cook was Vera, who specialised in steak and kidney pie and sponge puddings. Most members changed into formal dress for the bar. The Captain was deemed to be a person of some importance, and usually had a lunch party on Sundays for up to 12 people, at which he always paid for the wine. If you were asked to join the Captain's table, you felt you had been accepted.

Golf in the evenings was quite popular, and on some bank holidays there were occasional unofficial competitions where there were as many as six in a side. Participants played the same ball consecutively for between 6 and 9 holes with each team member having one club, and having to play in the same sequence.

John remembers an amusing story about a prominent member called Billy Betts, who had a caddy each weekend. When playing in a single club competition, Betts forgot to tell the caddy he was not wanted, so the caddy carried the one club for 18 holes! At that time, caddies were always available if required.

Lorna Peters (1909-2000)

Lorna joined the Club in 1946, being proposed by Ian Robb. She and her father were both members of Old Ford Manor Golf Club at Barnet. They joined Highgate to save petrol – still rationed for some time after the war. She recollected lady members were restricted as to when they could play golf: at weekends they could play only on Sunday afternoons – and then only with a man. Mixed foursomes were popular, and there was often a supper party in the evening. She remembered that the New Year's Eve dance (black tie) was well attended and music was always provided by a band.

The Ladies' Captain's Day was an important event in the calendar. Lorna remembered that, on one occasion, when the Club Secretary was absent, the Steward had far too much to drink and chased the Lady Captain with a bread knife – and had to be restrained.

Lorna was the Club Secretary of the Ladies section for 10 years from 1949, and remembers having a tremendous row with one of the crusty old committee members, who maintained that unmarried ladies were not entitled to a copy of the Club accounts. He phoned her the next day to apologise for his behaviour and to say they could, of course, have a copy. It is an interesting example of attitudes at that time.

Member Jenny Winn writes:

‘ Lorna was the Highgate Lady Captain twice, in 1961 and 1969, and was thrilled to be the first female President of the Club. At her fiftieth birthday, all her friends said she would never make single figures – but she came down to 7.

Lorna was Secretary of the English Ladies Golf Association for 10 years and organised all the National Championships – working from home as ELGA did not have offices of their own. She was also a founder of the ELGA Trust, which raises money to support and train young golfers. A great many players in the

Back (LtoR): Miss Gillian Hickson, *Secretary;* Mrs. Sue Hargreaves, *Assistant Secretary;*
Front: Mrs. Mary Roberts, *Chairman;* Mrs. Jane Honey, *Vice Chairman;* Mrs. Mary Clark, *Secretary Yorkshire L.C.G.A;*
Miss Lorna Peters **M.B.E.**, *President;* Mrs. Spencer, *Ladies Captain.* Otley G.C. The Town Mayor and Mayoress of Otley.

Lorna Peters, pictured here in the centre on the group attending the opening of the ELGA office in 1981, was awarded the MBE for services to golf.

Curtis and Solheim Cups have reason to be grateful to Lorna for financial help at the start of their careers. She used to meet players at the airport when they returned from international competitions and always encouraged them, and a large number had a great deal of respect and affection for her.

She was a Life President of ELGA, the LGU and Middlesex, and continued to support the county until she could no longer travel. She was awarded the MBE for her services to amateur golf.

Despite all these achievements, she remained very modest and unassuming, but anything she had to say was well worth listening to. One of the main reasons for my accepting the Middlesex captaincy was that Lorna would not have been pleased if I had turned it down!

The Wilkinson Gallery

The Wilkinson family was significant in the history of the Club. Norman Wilkinson, born in 1878, was a renowned marine artist and inventor of a new form of painted camouflage for ships. In 1924, he built the house in Sheldon Avenue to the left of the Club's drive. The house was built on the site of a duck pond. Norman built two fish ponds in the garden, which were fed by water draining from the course.

Norman was Men's Captain in 1934, and his wife, Eva, was Ladies' Captain in 1938. Their son, Rodney, was born in 1924 and was also a member of the Club, from 1932 to 1967. His watercolours of the course, which feature in this book, were painted in 1945.

Norman Wilkinson was awarded an OBE for his work in the Royal Navy, and Rodney received the MC and was mentioned in Despatches during his service in the Second World War.

Rodney Wilkinson

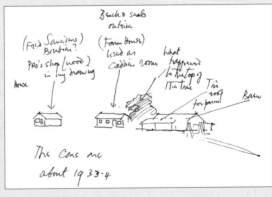

Top: the Wilkinsons on the present 3rd green in the 1930s. Above: from the Wilkinsons' garden looking towards the clubhouse – with annotated drawing by Rodney.

Left: Rodney's painting of the family home - called The End House because Sheldon Avenue finished there before the 1940s.

Below left: fly-fishing practice in the garden.

Below right: Norman at an exhibition.

Driving him crazy: the drive-in is stressful enough for any Captain, so spare a thought for L.G. Lancaster in 1951, who was faced with the humorous gift of a slightly irregular driver.

5 *THE GAME*

CLUB COMPETITIONS

After 1904, there were senior and junior monthly medal competitions, the results of which appeared on a regular basis in the local newspaper. In February 1905, the senior medal was won by Mr F. Homfray with a gross 89 less 8 = a net 81 and the junior medal was won by Mr G.H. Johnson with a 99 less 18 = 81. A year later, in March 1906, the winners were Mr Harold Wade with 82 less 10 = a net 72 and Mr C.L. Jones with a net 69.

In 1914, the net scores were still little changed; for instance in

February of that year, the winners were R.R. Shankland (clearly not handicapped by his unfortunate surname) with 90 less 7 = a net 83 and H.W. Edmunds with 97 less 14 = a net 83.

Apart from the fact that the course was still relatively new, it should be remembered, when considering these scores, that hickory clubs were still widely used. Anyone who has come across hickories will be aware that they are much more difficult to use than modern clubs. Also, the gutta-percha golf ball, which had been introduced circa 1850, was still being used in the early years of the 20th

83

Historic victories: reports of two matches against Hampstead in 1914, and the 1909 Ladies' Open meeting.

century. This was superseded by the rubber-cored ball, introduced by the Goodrich Rubber Company. As golf became a more popular game, so golf equipment developed, with the result that the scores of amateur club golfers improved rapidly over the years.

By 1914, the Club had various other competitions for which there were cups and trophies, and these included:

• Scratch Medal.

• Boxing Day Competition.

• Bogey Competition.

• Blakey Challenge Bowl (36 holes).

• Reid Cup.

• Captain's Prize.

• Lyle Cup (36-hole medal).

By 1940, the Club competitions were:

• The President's Prize.

• The Captain's Prize.

• The Potter Cup.

• The Club Prize.

GOLF

Kingsman swings Cup

DAVID KINGSMAN picked up Highgate's top trophy, the Scratch Cup at the club's annual dinner on Friday.

Mike Hoskins collected two awards, the Captain's prize and the Jock Gray Tankard along with partner James Bardner.

Another double winner was John Beer, who received the Highgate Cup and the Horns of Highgate trophy from Highgate captain Brian Burwash.

Other winners included Michael Steel (scratch medal); John Lloyd and Michael Isaacs (President's Prize); Mike Hartley and Nigel Solomon (Jubilee Foursomes); Martin Miller (Phoenix Trophy); Michael Hill (Whittington Trophy); Bill Jack (Bothams Cup); Colin Kerr (Veterans Cup); John Hall (Goodfellow Trophy) and Tom Bannon (Winter Knock-out).

Guests included Ivor Hall (Hampstead captain), Murray Corns (North Middlesex) and Metropolitan Police Commander Malcolm Campbell.

● Highgate winners . . . Michael Hill (left), David Kingsman and Mike Hoskins with captain Brian Burwash.

Making headlines: trophy time for some familiar faces (Michael Hill, David Kingsman, Captain Brian Burwash, Mike Hoskins) at the Men's Dinner in 1992.

- Elliott Challenge Cup (abandoned in 1964).

- The Lyle Cup (36-hole medal, abandoned in 1964).

- The Veterans Cup.

- The Goodfellow Bowl.

- The Victory Shield (presented by the 1918 President and Captain, as their competitions were not played during the First World War. Abandoned in 1964).

- The Highgate Cup.

- The Drage Prize.

- The Australia Cup (see Chapter 6).

- The Final of Medals (abandoned in 1964).

- The Scratch Cup.

- The Whitsun Bowl.

- *Daily Telegraph* Competition.

- The Staff Cup.

- Mixed Foursomes.

- The Phillips Cup (abandoned in 1964).

• The Horns of Highgate (inaugurated by the Captain Mr R. D. Bain in 1934).

Sixty-four years later, we compete for:

Men's Competitions:

• Scratch Cup (1966). Given by the Prime Minister of Malaysia, The Tunku Abdul Rahman (see Chapter 6).

• Scratch Medal (1971). Cup presented by R.C. Rowland Clark (Captain 1966).

• Captain's Prize (1948). No cup. Best 16 from the May medal play in matchplay knockout.

• President's Prize (1948). No cup. Foursomes matchplay knockout.

• Jubilee Foursomes (1954). No cup. Foursomes matchplay.

• Whittington Trophy (1966). Presented by Freddie Ferguson (Captain 1960) in 1965. Matchplay.

• Highgate Cup (1962). The best combined scores from the Horns of Highgate and Phoenix competitions. Presented by Mrs Madge Ferguson in 1962 to replace the cup lost in the second fire.

• Horns of Highgate. A small (replica) cup won by Mr Croft in 1936 and subsequently given to the Club. A combined competition

with the Old Cholmeleians who have their own cup. Tony Haskins gave a Horns memento in 1995.

• Phoenix Putter. Given by the then Captain, John Belsham, to commemorate the 1962 fire. The competition "would take the place of the Australia Cup which was now out of date" (per committee minutes). Strokeplay.

• Jock Gray Tankard (1964). Foursomes Bogey. Given by W.A. Gray, a Captain in the thirties.

• Veterans Cup (1934). Presented by Ernest Shaw. Singles knockout for members aged over 60.

• George Whipple Salver (1974). Two rounds of Stableford over the Easter weekend.

• Winter Knockout. Gary Player putter given by Tuffie Lapiner. Five eighths of the handicap difference used to allow the higher handicap player to start "holes up".

• Soutten Trophy. Presented by Col. A.C. Soutten MC (Secretary 1930 to 1950). Strokeplay.

• Winter Foursomes League (1966). Final 16 play in knockout.

• Captain and Professional's Challenge. Foursomes played on Sunday mornings.

• Botham's Trophy (1966). Presented

Up to scratch: the winning Highgate team in the MCGU Inter-Club Scratch Foursomes. Left to right: Meacher, Aljoe, Wells, Bax, Yates, Lloyd, Moxon and Crompton.

by Arnold Botham. Knockout singles for handicaps 11 to 19.

• Past Captain's Salver (1985). Presented by Tom Webster. Stableford.

• Senior Salver (1986). Presented by John Pollock. Stableford for members over 50.

• Senior Tankard. Stableford for members over 50.

• Rabbits Trophy (1970). Presented by John Salisse. Knockout for handicaps between 19 and 28.

• Goodfellow Trophy (1939). Presented by Magnus Goodfellow. Cup replaced after the 1962 fire. Five clubs or less strokeplay.

• Five Day Members Trophy (1993). Presented by Sir John Boynton. Stableford.

Mixed Competitions

• The Forester Salver (1971). Given by Mr and Mrs Forester. Mixed greensomes.

• The Sutherland Cup (1973).

High standards: Eva Wilkinson, Ladies Captain in 1938, kept records of some impressively low handicaps (top) and did well in the September medal (above).

Winn in for two at the 7th

A number of members have holes-in-one every year, but one feat unlikely to be repeated took place in the mid-sixties when Michael Winn (Captain in 1982) had an albatross two at the 7th hole (more than 520 yds). After a major drive, he hit a majestic brassie. Michael and his partner looked for the ball around the green and eventually found it in the cup. It was witnessed by his partner, Guy Lancaster, and also a player who was on the 9th tee at the time. Michael (pictured left) has since died, but a tree alongside the 7th fairway bears his name and marks a remarkable golfing achievement at Highgate.

Presented by John Belsham (Captain 1962/63). Husband and wife mixed foursomes.

• Mixed Foursomes (1954). Cup presented by Joyce Hopson in 1990.

Ladies' Competitions

• Barrett Cup (1925). Formerly the Hospital Cup. Strokeplay.

• Cancer Relief Spoon. Stableford.

• Captain's Prize (1919).

• Coronation Salver (1953). Three best Stableford scores, Mar-Sept.

• Winter and Summer Eclectic. Silver and bronze divisions.

• Middlesex Eclectic.

• Erica De Courcey Cup. Replaced the former Winter League competition in 2000.

- Goodfellow Cup (1929). Eight best in May medal play matchplay knockout.

- Grannie's Mug.

- Harris Browne Bowl (1911). Matchplay knockout.

- Junior Prize (1962). Matchplay knockout, bronze division.

- Kit's Cup. Stableford, 55+ years.

- Ledger Cup (1919).

- Winter Knockout. Matchplay.

- Lorna Peters Stableford Trophy (1999).

- Marcia's Memento. Stableford. Donated by Marcia Schlief on her return to the United States.

- Middlesex Five Club Knockout.

It's a fact

Harry Vardon was reported as visiting the club on 2 November 1907 for a 36-hole match against "the best ball" but the result cannot be traced . . .

In 1970, four members who had attended the men's dinner were still playing cards at 4 o'clock in the morning. The committee ruled that the clubhouse would close 30 minutes after the bar had shut.

- Noor Bowl (1966). Donated by Colonel Mohamed and Mrs Iaisaha Noor on their return to Malaysia. Strokeplay.

- Palma Dulciana (Past Captain's Foursomes, 1995). Knockout foursomes played over two weekends.

- Past Lady Captain's Trophy.

- President's Prize. Stableford.

- Ridgewell Cup (1930). 36-hole strokeplay.

- Scratch Medal (1988). 36 holes.

- Scratch Trophies (1962). Silver and bronze division summer matchplay knockout.

- Senior/Junior Foursomes (1962). Senior plays with junior in balloted matchplay knockout.

- Slowe Cup (1971). Past Captains. Best net score at Spring Meeting.

- Sunday Players Trophy (1962). Matchplay knockout.

- Vera Lancaster Trophy (1973). Foursomes stableford.

- Veterans Trophy (1960). Matchplay knockout for 60+.

Inter-Club Matches

The Club is affiliated to the Middlesex County Golf Union. In

1970, Richard Hayward and George Rothman won the MCGU Rowse Trophy. The Club was successful again in 1985 when David Kingsman and John Lloyd participated. Since that time, the competition format has been changed to a team event of 10 players, and Highgate were the losing finalists in 1999 and 2002.

Middlesex Inter-Club team championship (six-a-side): the Club was the winner in 1980, 1984 and 1987, and finalist in 1979.

The Foxes Competition

In September 1967, committee member Tony Pepper suggestsed that Highgate join the North London Foxes Competition. It was agreed that the Club would join Finchley, Hampstead, Hendon and North Middlesex for the 1968 season.

The annual programme consists of home and away matches played mid-week during the summer months, with spring and autumn meetings. These events are always very convivial and are followed by a supper. The 25th anniversary of our joining was celebrated with a dinner at Highgate in 1993 at which John Salisse presided and Ian Wallace, always a keen supporter, also spoke and later sang to the enjoyment of all present.

The Tuesday Evening Champagne Competition

Joan Spencer tells the story:

' This 9-hole competition was started in 1981 by Annette O'Gorman, assisted by a few other members and encouraged by the then Lady Captain, Hilda Jones. Since that time, it has become increasingly popular and has assisted the trend towards the ladies' and men's sections becoming more integrated.

The competition runs from 5pm until dark throughout the summer months. Players can just turn up and are found a partner. For many years, this has been followed by a supper for those who wish to stay. Over the past few years, 70% of the participants have stayed for supper.

Since 1985, many local charities have been supported, including Hill Homes, The North London Hospice, The Sick Children's Trust, Harrington Scheme, School for Children with Cerebral Palsy and

It's a fact

The best recorded score by a lady is Lulu Housman's gross 70 (net 64) returned on 7 July 2003.

On the boards

Above left: Past and present Men's Captains, Presidents and Chairmen*:

Henry Minto, Morton Pollock, Brian Adams, Mike Hoskins, Tony Mackintosh, John Bardner, Steve Morris, Bill Jack, Pat Ridett, John Beer, Ralph Riddell-Carre, John Pollock, Roger Lane, John Radcliffe, John Salisse, David Booth, John Drew, Richard Grindall, John Chaumeton, Tim Chapman, Raymond Ferry, Nick Moore, James Henry, John Hall, Bert Brant and Mike Hartley.

Below left: Ladies' Captains*:

Christiane Duckworth, Eileen Phillips, Pat Hone, Annette O'Gorman, Sue Chapman, Debbie Dutton, Sally Walsh, Joan Spencer, Elsie Morton, Heidi Corsi, Ann

Pollock, Cassie Ross, Jenny Winn, Rose Bardner, Margot Parfitt, Helen Radcliffe, Margaret Brant.

Inset: Brian Burwash, Martin Miller, Michael McFee, Ted Russell, Sue Miller and Evelyn Lyons.

Above: a less formal gathering (top) eventually collapses into humour.

* Not all of the officers were present, or could provide a photograph.

Matt Deal (front centre) celebrates the setting of a new course record on 13 October 2002, while playing in the Three Pros tournament (Highgate, Hampstead and Hendon).

various local hospital initiatives. The charity is chosen by the two Captains, and, since 1985, £19,500 has been raised in small donations and by way of raffles.

The last night of the season in September is very popular and involves a special supper. The most unusual last night competition was an illuminated 8-hole competition sponsored by Bernard Gallagher. On that occasion, the supper was eaten first and then the golf was played in the dark with an illuminated ball, which had a fluorescent green core. It could easily be followed through the air but was incredibly difficult to hit. Two balls per person were allowed but none were lost in the rough because they were easily spotted. The

Hole	Marker's Score	White Yards	Par	Yellow Yards	Stroke Index	Score A	Score B	W = + L = - H = 0 Points	Red Yards	Par	Stroke Index
1		296	4	272	13	4			284	4	13
2		322	4	308	9	4			305	4	9
3		384	4	352	5	3			349	4	3
4		117	3	106	17	3			113	3	17
5		337	4	321	11	4			322	4	11
6		462	4	439	1	3			407	4	1
7		521	5	500	7	4			472	5	7
8		154	3	134	15	3			123	3	15
9		440	4	437	3	5			403	5	5
OUT		3033	35	2868		33			2778	36	

PLEASE AVOID SLOW PLAY AT ALL TIMES

Hole	Marker's Score	White Yards	Par	Yellow Yards	Stroke Index	Score A	Score B	W = + L = - H = 0 Points	Red Yards	Par	Stroke Index
10		366	4	346	14	4			333	4	14
11		197	3	187	8	3			164	3	8
12		278	4	266	16	3			263	4	16
13		351	4	336	4	4			306	4	6
14		376	4	350	10	4			346	4	4
15		443	4	417	2	4			415	5	10
16		470	4	456	6	3			416	4	2
17		151	3	126	18	1			110	3	18
18		320	4	320	12	4			308	4	12
IN		2952	34	2804		30			2661	35	
OUT		3033	35	2868		33			2778	36	
TOTAL		5985	69	5672		63			5439	71	

COMPETITION 3 PRO'S MATCH **TIME**
DATE 13.10.02
Player A Matt Deal (Hendon)
Player B

Stableford Points or Par Result — HANDICAP — NETT

Marker's Signature — Player's signature — *M Deal*

How he did it: Matt Deal's record-breaking card of 63 included a hole-in-one at the 17th.

Course Records

Year	Amateur	Score	Professional	Score
1907			F. Saunders	71
1908			Albert Saunders	70
1909			P.C.B. Berisford	74
1910			C. Butchart	70
1911			W.H. Don	71
1912			Albert Saunders	69
1916			P.L. Smith	68
1924			W.H. Don	66
1928			C.A. Whitcombe	68
1929	Reservoir constructed – course remodelled			
1933			R.D. Knox	66
1936			R.D. Knox	67
1938	K.F. Baker	72	C.A. Whitcombe	68
1938			J.J. Taylor	68
1939	J. Grimditch	72	J. Ockenden	68
1940	R.D. Knox	72		
1952	J. Geils	70		
1968	L. Smith	68		
1984	D. Kingsman	66		
1985	P. Bax	66		
1986			Peter Alliss	68
1992	I. Martin	66		
1995	C. Lloyd	66		
1996			R. Turner	66
1998			L. Jones	65
2002			Matt Deal	63

Thirties style: a foursome from before the war.

course looked as if it were full of aircraft runways as there were lights at intervals down the centre of each fairway and on the flagsticks. The greens staff had been very busy laying them out. Each player had a light hanging down his or her back to minimise the dangers from players behind. This event was much enjoyed, and if the special golf balls can be obtained, the organisers would like to repeat it. Hopefully the Tuesday Champagne competition will continue for years to come. **9**

Annette O'Gorman comments:

6 At our champagne party in 1983, we had a wonderful evening. Ian Wallace (now an honorary member), well known from the programme *My Music* entertained

us royally. We were always well supported by Captains and committee members. I remember joking in my speech about our then President saying he was so rich that when he was ill, the Inland Revenue sent him a Get Well card.

The following year, the Captain remarked 'This is your baby, Annette'. I was human enough to feel a little pleased with myself and on second thoughts a bit like an unmarried mother. However, I parried comments and questions on the subject by making three points.

1) The name of the father was never disclosed.

2) The baby didn't talk as much as the mother, and

3) When asked in the club 'are you having another?' I replied, 'No, it's the way I've got my coat buttoned up'.

I was proud to be in at the birth of the baby champagne competition (which, by the way, was adopted), but more proud to see how, under Joan's guidance, it has grown into such a healthy child. **"**

Another recent innovation is the Thursday morning **Swindlers Competition.**

One of the organisers, **Tony Halstead**, comments as follows:

" When Viv Shore was elected Chairman of the Club in 1994, he noticed a growing number of members – either five day, newly retired or fortunate enough to be able to take time off from work – looking for a game of golf. He realised it was difficult to get to know other Club members when you could only play midweek.

Viv persuaded one of his regular partners, Ron Menozzi, to organise a Highgate Swindlers competition. A Thursday morning tee-off time was booked, a notice went up, and on the first Thursday, six members turned up.

Now, each week, an average of 35 play, and during the year well over 100 members will have played at least once – many playing between 20 and 30 rounds. There is a £3 fee, and start times are from 8.45 to 9.15.

Ron Menozzi sadly died after running and organising the Swindlers for three years. His place has been taken over time by Bob Trew, myself, Arthur Franks and Stephen Albert.

The weekly competition is a Stableford played off the yellow tees. The winner receives a modest cash sum, the balance of the fund going towards the 'Swindlers bar drink' and a charity chosen by the members.

To give everyone a chance of winning, handicaps are adjusted. From January 1 each year, all members play off their club handicap. Any score of 38 points and more secures a reduction in the member's handicap – this is calculated by deducting a stroke for every two points over 36. The competition got its name because a cunning fellow – or swindler – would be careful not to score 40 points early in the season!

Records of each round are recorded on computer and the player who records the best 15 rounds during the year is presented with an engraved tankard at the Christmas lunch; their name is also engraved on the salver on display in the trophy cabinet.

In 1994, Ann Pollock, the Ladies Captain, suggested a twice-yearly challenge between the Swindlers and the Ladies. In May and October, a highly competitive match is fought for the Menozzi Cup, after which as many as 70 members sit down for a friendly lunch. **'**

It is a truism that no organisation remains unchanged. Over the decades, one of the glories of HGC is that there have never been starting times at weekends, apart from competitions, and, on weekend mornings, members could come to the Club unfixed and arrange a game, usually a fourball, with no problem. Sometimes there might be 10 or more fourballs out on the course on Saturday and Sunday mornings. After the war, and right up until the early 1990s, it was the practice for the Captain to meet, and in effect interview, prospective new members over a drink after 12 o'clock on Sunday mornings.

The Captain was usually playing in his regular fourball during the morning, and, in those days, other fours automatically stood aside to allow the Captain and his group through. In this way, he could be certain of being back in the clubhouse on time.

Over the past few years, the number of members turning up unfixed on weekend mornings seems to have diminished, but a new initiative by Captains John Hall and David Booth has sought to address the situation.

The Saturnalians meet on the practice putting green at 12 o'clock on Saturdays and have a structured programme over the winter and summer periods. This grouping has proved to be increasingly popular in recent times.

A tip from the top: Magnus Goodfellow, who gave his name to our limited clubs competition, swings into action.

Malaysian matchmakers: Captain Ken Howden receives the trophy from the Captain of the RASGS team.

6 HOME & AWAY

The Malaysian Connection

The Committee minutes of September 1965 mention a match against the Selangor Golf Society.

John Salisse comments:

‘From the early sixties until 1985, a match between a HGC team and the Royal Alam Shah Golfing Society (RASGS) took place at Highgate every two or three years. The event usually took place on Sunday afternoons, and was followed by a black tie dinner in the clubhouse.

This was always a very convivial event, and at the dinner in 1980 their Captain said it was time we had a return match in Malaysia. The home team chortled, but I said I would organise a team and I was true to my word.

A group of about 12 of us, plus four female partners, flew to Malaysia in 1985. We stayed at the Hilton Hotel just outside Kuala Lumpur – near the Subang National Golf Club – and we had the free use of a bus kindly provided by our hosts.

After some practice rounds, the fourball match took place early one morning (it was hot and very humid) and we lost 4 and 2. Following the game, an excellent buffet lunch was provided in a marquee.

Two evenings later, an official golf club reception and dinner was held at the Hilton, organised by our hosts

Malaysian match: the 1988 HGC and RASGS teams gather at Highgate.

and attended by about 200 people. Everyone on the top table had a gold plate in front of them – ranging from very large (in front of the Sultan) down to fairly small (the Prime Minister's). As the Highgate Captain, I sat on the top table with his Royal Highness, his daughter and various dignitaries. The Sultan presented mugs and other prizes to our team and I responded appropriately with a formal speech, the contents of which I had previously discussed with our embassy.

A few nights later, we attended a state banquet at the Sultan's palace. This event was held to commemorate his jubilee, and approximately 2,000 attended. It ended with a massive firework display. This was the final event of our visit and we were very honoured to be included. The Highgate party then dispersed to Hong Kong, Australia and to other destinations before returning to the UK. **'**

Raymond Ferry takes up the story of the Malaysian connection:

' In 1988, RASGS returned to London. Our captain was Tony Pepper, who steered Highgate to victory and repossession of the SSG trophy. For various reasons, the return match in Kuala Lumpur, scheduled for early 1989, failed to materialise. Presently the SSG Trophy languishes uncontested in the Highgate trophy cabinet.

Tony Pepper was eagerly anticipating leading Highgate to victory in Kuala Lumpur, to repeat his performance of the early fifties, when he played a slightly different role. Tony had served as a National Service subaltern with the 13/18th Royal Hussars in a successful jungle campaign against communist insurgents.

Highgate's connection with Malaysia goes back further than the RASGS matches. Among our members in the fifties and sixties were The Tunku Abdul Rahman, Prime Minister of Malaysia. His official residence was near the 13th tee, and we are indebted to him for the gift of the beautifully designed Scratch Cup. Also among the members was the Indonesian ambassador, and this posed something of a potential problem, as a state of hostilities existed at the time between Malaysia and Indonesia.

Each of these VIP members played golf at Highgate in the company of a large entourage, and every effort was made by the club to avoid any sort of diplomatic incident on the course (or elsewhere).

'

The Australia Cup

The Australia Cup was contested during an annual evening competition, which was followed by a dinner. The cup itself was presented in 1920 by a large group of Australian members of the Club in appreciation of the hospitality they had received.

The Australia Cup was still being played for in the fifties, but fell into disuse and later was superseded by the America Cup. While it was still an active competition, Highgate had a reciprocal arrangement with the Australian Golf Club in Sydney. The centenary history of that club, published in 1982, mentions the presentation of the Australia Cup to Highgate, and also that, in, 1931, Highgate presented the Australian Golf Club with the Highgate Cup. It was only in the sixties that this competition was withdrawn from the AGC's diary because of the club's overfull programme.

One consequence of this connection was that the Australian Test cricketers used to play golf at Highgate. One member, Guy Lancaster, remembers shaking hands with the legendary Don Bradman when he was in the UK for the 1948 Test series.

Rodney Wilkinson, who lived at 43 Sheldon Avenue – the house that backs on to the 5th green – remembers one specific Aussie encounter.

He was in the garden on a Sunday afternoon and heard a ball go into the hedge, so went round to help locate it. He saw a fourball approaching, with four caddies, and it transpired that the wayward shot had been hit by Don Bradman. He was playing with three other Australian cricketers, all then in the middle of the Lord's Test Match.

The original cup was presumably destroyed in the 1926 fire, but quite by chance the Club became aware that, in November 2001, a duplicate was up for sale at a furniture auction in Essex. The Club was lucky enough to be able to purchase this trophy, dated 12 July 1922. The Cup had been won by Club member Mr W. Adamson, who then lived at 5 Fordington Road.

Some research was carried out and it turned out that the cup was put into the auction by the 76-year-old son of the winner. He was aware that his father had been given the duplicate by the Club to keep as he had won the competition three years running – presumably from its inception.

This Australia Cup competition was cancelled in 1963 as the committee considered it "to be out of date". Currently a match against the AGC in Sydney in February 2005 is under consideration.

The Old Chomeleians

Highgate School has had a long association with Highgate Golf Club, dating back to the inauguration of the Old Cholmeleian Club in 1906. The connection seems to have fluctuated over the years, but is still close. The Horns of Highgate competition and ceremony still causes much amusement.

John Scott (OC and HGC member of long standing) comments on the story of this distinguished organisation:

'The Old Cholmeleian Golfing Society came into being in 1906 with the playing of a knockout competition for the Francis Challenge Cup. This competition was open to both former pupils and masters of Highgate School.

There were 42 entrants for the first

competition, of whom at least six were masters at the school. The winner was P.R. Lurcott.

In 1907, the competition was again contested, and once again the winner was P.R. Lurcott, who kept the Francis Challenge Cup.

This competition has been played for annually ever since, except for the interruption of the two world wars.

From 1908 to 1911, there was no cup for the winner, but, in 1912, E.H. Kelly, the Headmaster of the Junior School, presented the Kelly Cup, which is still contested for today.

In 1907, the Cholmeleians held a strokeplay competition at Northwood Golf Club and in the following year played their first match. This was against Highgate Golf Club on 15 July 1908 and Highgate won 9-1.

In July 1909, the OCs beat Highgate Golf Club 8-4. This was only one of two recorded occasions on which the OCs had beaten the Golf Club.

Between 1910 and 1914, there were annual matches held in July between Highgate GC and OCs. The OCs drew in 1912 and lost the others.

In the eight years between its foundation and the coming of the Great War, the Cholmeleians had established a golfing framework which organised an annual knockout competition for its members.

As with most things in Britain, Cholmeleian golf was very different in the aftermath of the Great War. It took some years for the Golf Society to get organised, but, in 1921, they began playing for the Kelly Cup once again. The competition was played with a different format, with a qualifying round played at Highgate and the best four scores moving into a knockout competition. The winner in 1921 was G.S. Clarkson.

The new format continued for many years with the qualifying round being played at Highgate until it moved to Old Ford Manor in 1928 and subsequently to Hadley Wood, before returning to Highgate in 1937. In 1938, the qualifiers were taken from the top scores in the Horns of Highgate competition.

After the Great War, there were no matches against Highgate Golf Club until 1933 (the 25th anniversary of the first match) when Highgate GC won 5-4. These matches continued up to 1939, with a victory for the Cholmeleians in 1938. It is interesting to note that G.C. Macmillan played for Highgate Golf Club both in this match and in the original match in 1908. He won his singles matches both times, playing right-handed in 1908, then left-handed in 1938 because of a war injury.

Relations between the Society and the Club had been further cemented in 1934 when the Club and the Society took part in the first Horns of Highgate competition. A.J.M. Young was the Cholmeleian winner, with F.G. Jewell winning in 1935. In those days, the winner was given a small silver cup as a memento, and, thanks to Freddy Jewell's generosity, his cup is presented annually to the Old Chomeleian winner.

Another gesture of friendship was shown in June 1936 when the committee of Highgate GC decided to admit, without payment of entrance fee, ex-scholars of Highgate School under 24 years of age who were recommended by the Old Cholmeleian Golfing Society.

Thanks to the initiative of our forefathers and the fact that Highgate School is now a day school, it seems that Club and Society will be forever firm friends with a large joint membership. **,**

Left: the replica of the Australia Cup.

History of Highgate Cup

HISTORY OF HIGHGATE CUP

We recently received correspondence from John Chaumeton, Member of The Highgate Golf Club and personal friend of Mr and Mrs Whalley, which contains historical information regarding the Highgate Cup.

Members may be interested to read excerpts from Mr Chaumeton's letter to our Captain:

"Dear Arthur,

The Cup in question was given in 1920 to Highgate Golf Club by some of your Countrymen who were Members at that time and we reciprocated by giving to your Club in 1930 The Highgate Cup which I understand was withdrawn from your match programme in, I think, 1967.

We have had 2 major fires, in 1926 and 1962, in which all our silverware melted down so we were very pleased to obtain this Cup at auction. I have ascertained that it was sold by the 76 year old son of the Winner in 1922. The reason it is a Duplicate is that the Winner, Mr W Adamson, won it from inception, and for the following 2 years, and he was given this Duplicate Cup to keep in recognition of this feat.

The connection between our Clubs goes back a long time, as mentioned in your History Book "Ten Decades", particularly on pages 45 and 144.

Yours sincerely,
John Chaumeton"

6 The Australian Golf Club

The cup stands 14" tall and has inscribed on it:

Highgate Golf Club
The Australia Cup (Replica)
Won by Mr W. Adamson 12 July 1922.

Above: the Australian Golf Club in Sydney reports on the discovery of the trophy.

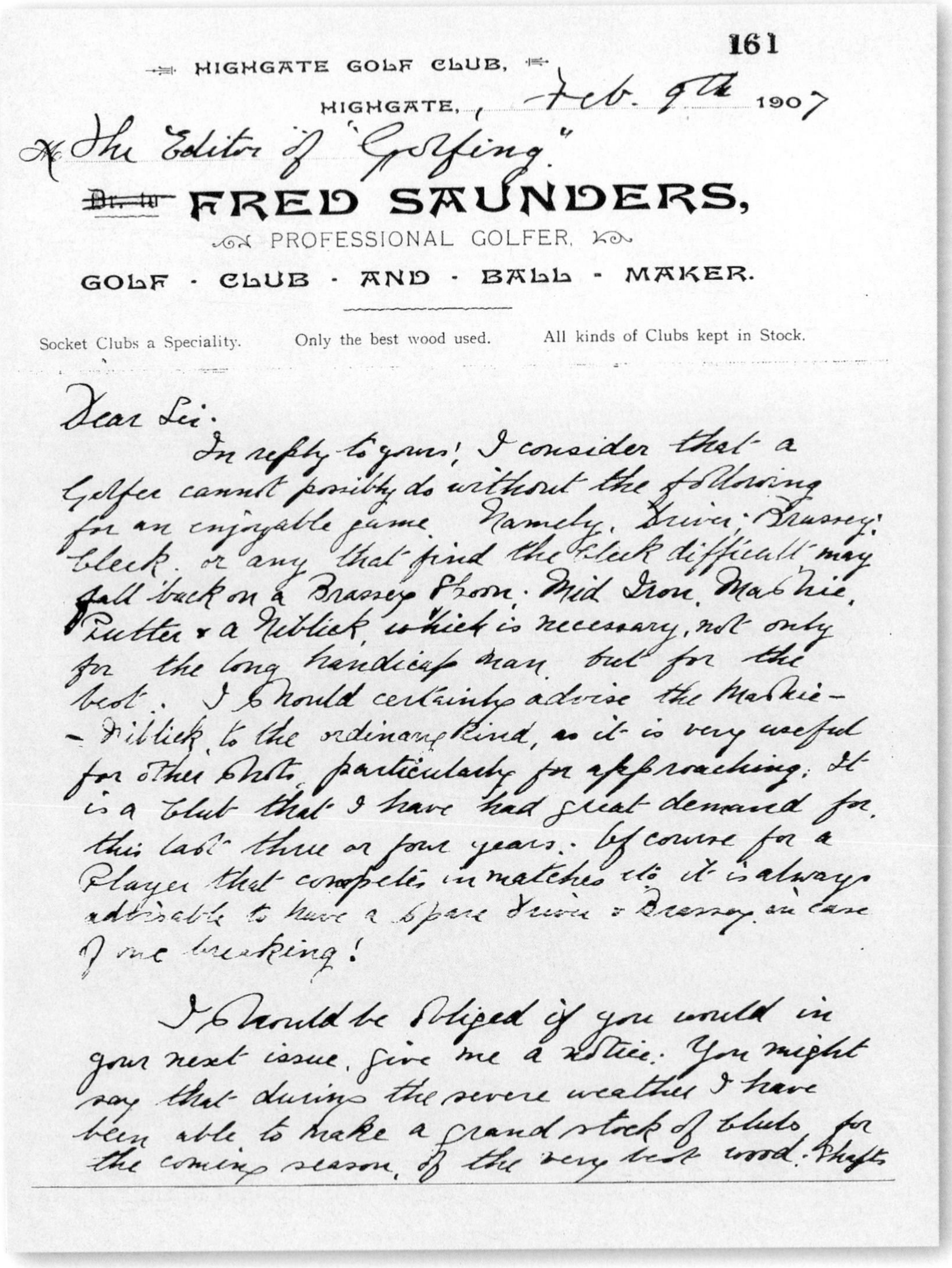

161

⇥ HIGHGATE GOLF CLUB, ⇤

HIGHGATE, *Feb. 9th* 1907

The Editor of "Golfing"

FRED SAUNDERS,

⚘ PROFESSIONAL GOLFER, ⚘

GOLF · CLUB · AND · BALL · MAKER.

Socket Clubs a Speciality.   Only the best wood used.   All kinds of Clubs kept in Stock.

Dear Sir,

In reply to yours, I consider that a Golfer cannot possibly do without the following for an enjoyable game. Namely, Driver, Brassey, Cleek, or any that find the Cleek difficult may fall back on a Brassey Spoon. Mid Iron, Mashie, Putter & a Niblick, which is necessary, not only for the long handicap man, but for the best. I should certainly advise the Mashie-Niblick to the ordinary kind, as it is very useful for other shots, particularly for approaching. It is a club that I have had great demand for, this last three or four years. Of course for a Player that competes in matches &c it is always advisable to have a spare Driver & Brassey, in case of one breaking!

I should be obliged if you would in your next issue, give me a notice. You might say that during the severe weather I have been able to make a grand stock of clubs for the coming season, of the very best wood. Shafts

Propaganda pro: Fred Saunders shares his wisdom with the editor of Golfing *magazine.*

7 *THE PROS*

In this chapter we look back over the careers of the professionals at Highgate Golf Club.

C. S. Butchart (HGC professional 1904).

Butchart was born at Carnoustie in 1876 and, as already mentioned, helped with the original design of the course. He was the professional at many clubs, including Berlin Golf Club (1911-1914) and Baltimore Golf Club in the USA (1921).

He ended his career as a well-known course designer in the States. He died in 1955.

Fred Saunders (professional 1905-1937).

Fred Saunders was born in Devon in 1876 and was an assistant to Charles Gibson at Westward Ho! before taking up the pro's job at Handsworth in Birmingham in 1897. He moved from there to Highgate in 1905 and spent the rest of his career with the Club. He became a well-known club maker and patented one club called the Straight Line Putter, of which the Club has a sample. Saunders produced these with an aluminium head, featuring an aiming line on a lobe at the rear of the club. He also produced a range of hickory-shafted irons and woods.

Groundbreaker: C.S. Butchart in action. He became a well-respected golf course designer.

Saunders had a reputation as an accomplished singer with a booming bass voice, which was apparently heard at many Club functions.

In 1910, the official organ of the Professional Golfers' Association was *Golf Illustrated*, and, in its edition of 18 March 1910, the following report appeared:

❝ Fred Saunders, the Highgate Club's professional, is the possessor of a highly trained voice,

FRED SAUNDERS

Practical Golf Club Maker and Expert Instructor

Highgate Golf Club
HIGHGATE, LONDON, N.

Special Diploma awarded for Left-Handed Clubs at Deal Exhibition, 1919

ALSO

Three Diplomas for Driver, Brassie, & Putter at St. Andrews Exhibition, 1910

Use Saunders'

DRIVERS, BRASSIES, & IRON CLUBS

The Best on the Market

FRED SAUNDERS, Highgate G.C., Highgate, London, N.

799

Forging a reputation: Fred Saunders was a tireless promoter of his wares. Pictured below right is a selection of his clubs, including the famous "straight line" putter.

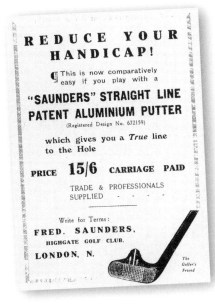

REDUCE YOUR HANDICAP!

This is now comparatively easy if you play with a

"SAUNDERS" STRAIGHT LINE PATENT ALUMINIUM PUTTER

(Registered Design No. 672159)

which gives you a *True* line to the Hole

PRICE **15/6** CARRIAGE PAID

TRADE & PROFESSIONALS SUPPLIED - - -

Write for Terms:
FRED. SAUNDERS,
HIGHGATE GOLF CLUB.
LONDON, N.

The Golfer's Friend

an accomplishment all the more peculiar seeing that golf professionals as a rule are not musical. I will admit that one member is supposed to equal George Elliot at coon singing – but I have heard him, much to my sorrow – while another frequently murders 'A Jovial Monk' and makes the night hideous by retailing the sorrows of 'A Bedouin Love Song', generally finishing up the evening, and the audience, by singing the 'Bandolero'. For the benefit of those who occasionally have, much against their wills, to listen to this operatic star, I may say he has lately added to his repertoire Kipling's 'On the Road to Mandalay': may he soon take that road never to return. It would be a fitting fate, especially as he further contemplates annoying people with 'Asleep in the Deep'. An epitaph on his tombstone of Asleep in the Deep on the Road to Mandalay would read well. Let him and his unfortunate audience take warning.**'**

The publication *Compendium of British Club Makers* backs up the claims for Saunders' booming bass. His nickname in Gibson's shop at Westward Ho! was 'he of the voice'.

Tom Pierpoint (professional 1937-1941). He joined the RAF and was killed on a bombing raid over Germany in 1942. His brother was Albert Pierpoint, a publican and also the last hangman in Britain.

W. Cole (professional 1947-1950).

P. Baverstock (professional 1950-1954).

F. S. Boobyer (professional 1954-1963).

Laurie Ayton (professional 1963-1974).

Laurie Ayton came from an old golfing family. The committee noted that he was to play in the Open at Carnoustie in 1960.

A member recollected one story about him.

'Laurie Ayton was proud of his good looks, especially his fine head of white hair. After playing he would always take a shower and then make use of the jar of Brylcream, which, in those days, stood on a shelf in the locker room. One day, Alec, the then locker room attendant and a mischievous fellow, topped the jar up with a layer of Copydex. Immediately after using a lavish handful of this,

Spiked: Highgate pro Laurie Ayton was the victim of a practical joke in the locker room.

The assistant pro who lost out

Bill Sharpe was born in 1917 and was the assistant at Morecambe Golf Club, then worked under Pierpoint at Prestbury. When Pierpoint moved to Highgate, Sharpe came with him – he was then aged 20 and a scratch golfer.

He was the assistant pro at Highgate for a short period from May 1937. His remuneration was £2 per week. He remembered two prominent members who played golf every Saturday morning being Willie Idris (of the drinks firm) and Alfred Brandon, who had a chain of clothes stores. They played for £25 a time, which was a large amount in those days.

He remembers Pierpoint playing in two challenge matches. The first was against one Bert Rhodes, whom he beat over 72 holes. The second found him up against Eddie Whitcombe, who "overcame

him easily". Sharpe remembered one occasion when he played for money – or so he thought. A member came into the pro's shop and issued a challenge that he would back the son of the caddymaster, Mick Reddy, who had a handicap of +1 , for an amount of £25. Sharpe did not have any money, but another member overheard the discussion and backed him for the amount of the wager. Sharpe won, but the member did not share his winnings with the young assistant.

Sharpe used to give lessons for 2s/6d (12.5p) and would start his teaching as early as 6 o'clock in the morning. However, he found it very difficult financially and soon left.

In the war, he was a pilot in the RAF on Halifax bombers and survived many missions. He now lives in Penrith.

Laurie's hair dried into stiff spikes through which he could barely force his comb. The result was hilarious, with Laurie, when he discovered who had played the trick, chasing Alec round the locker room and then, swearing profusely, forcing him under one of the showers, but not before he had turned it fully on. **,**

Ayton was a well-liked Club professional although his shop left a little to be desired. He was still a very effective golfer, especially within 75 yards of the green.

Henry Arnott (professional 1974-1986).

Robin Turner (professional since 1986).

Following through: Fred Saunders demonstrates the correct way to finish.

Devastation: all that remained of the mixed lounge after the 1962 clubhouse fire.

8 THE FIRES

THE 1926 FIRE

The original clubhouse was substantially refurbished in 1925 and formally reopened on 11 March 1926. It must have been particularly galling for the Club that a serious fire substantially destroyed the building five months later.

The local newspaper reported on 21 July 1926:

> A fire broke out at the pavilion and clubhouse of the Highgate Golf Club during luncheon time on Wednesday and the building, which has only recently been reconstructed, was badly damaged. The flames, fanned by a strong wind, quickly spread, and the Hornsey and Finchley Fire Brigade were handicapped by the fact that there were no hydrants near the premises and their water supply had to be obtained from a distance. Some of the furniture was saved by members who were lunching in the clubhouse, but golf clubs and many personal belongings of members were destroyed.

It would appear that the original wooden structure was rapidly rebuilt, and a brick and tiled building was ready for use the next year.

THE 1962 FIRE

The second disastrous fire occurred

on the night of 29-30 June.

The local newspaper reported the following week:

'A clanging burglar alarm saved six lives when flames swept through Highgate Golf Club's pavilion early on Saturday morning.

The bell awoke the steward, Mr Thomas Holland, his wife Jean and their two children in their first-floor flat. Also sleeping in the building were the club steward's mother-in-law, Mrs Jean Ferguson, and resident cook, Miss May Cannings.

Bundling them to safety, Mr Holland gave the alarm. Firemen fought the blaze for over three hours but could not save the building. The roof caved in, virtually the whole of the building, including lockers containing hundreds of sets of golf clubs, was completely gutted, and damage is estimated at many thousands of pounds.

In his temporary office – a storage shed – the secretary of the 800-member club, Major James R. Adair, told *The Express and News* yesterday:

"The Club is still running and the club captain, Mr S.J. Belsham, and members of the committee are making every effort to ensure that full facilities are operating again as soon as possible. We are making temporary arrangements for the social side until full-scale reconstruction has been carried out." '

With commendable speed, Captain John Belsham organised the committee to meet the day after the fire and it was noted that all the Club records had been lost in the fire. It was agreed that the staff would continue to be paid and temporary accommodation would be provided for them.

At the next meeting, on 5 July, it was agreed that the professional's shop would be taken over as a bar (clearly they had the right priorities). The part of the clubhouse occupied by the ladies had not been damaged much and it was decided this would be weatherboarded so it could be fully utilised. It was decided to appoint a firm of assessors to negotiate with the insurers on behalf of the Club.

At the meeting on 11 July, it was agreed that a local builder should be approached regarding the rebuilding. Comment was made that the Loss of Revenue insurance cover was restricted to 75%. This was the first mention of problems on the insurance front.

On 28 July, an architect – Peter Ednie – was interviewed. The extent of insurance cover was considered. It

ENOUGH' | Golf club loss

Road pute

eek ship-owner's te brought pro- st Heath Road,

between £15,000 ities of neighbour- gh for West Heath 0.

ation for a change e site, the Lands t a nearby convent

a house in this road able plot at £30,000 ouses of this character ve been built and sold mes."

said: "In 1930 there houses in spacious at least an acre. In ation is that the large 930 have been turned r institutions of one other and that smaller h smaller plots have

unal's decision is ex- bout a month."

A clanging burglar alarm saved six lives when flames swept through Highgate golf club's pavilion early on Saturday morning.

The bell awoke resident steward Mr. Thomas Holland sleeping with his wife, Jean, and two children in their first-floor flat. Also sleeping in the building were the club stewardess—his mother-in-law, Mrs. Jean Ferguson—and resident cook Miss May Cannings.

Bundling them to safety, Mr. Holland gave the alarm. Firemen fought the blaze for over three hours but could not save the building.

The roof caved in, virtually the whole of the building, including lockers containing hundreds of sets of golf clubs, was completely gutted, and damage is estimated at many thou-

In his temporary office—a storage shed—the secretary of the 800-member club, Major James R. Adair, told the Express & News yesterday (Thursday): "The club is still running, and the club captain, Mr. S. J. Belsham, and members of the committee are making every effort to ensure that full facilities are operating again as soon as possible.

"We are making temporary arrangements for the social side until full-scale reconstruction has been carried out."

Families were evacuated from nearby houses as firemen fought a blaze at the Telefilm studios in Chalk Farm Road early on Sunday.

The studios, where filming had been going on until 10.20 the previous evening, were gutted. The blaze was spotted by passer-by Mr. Peter Coviello, of Belsize Park Gardens, Hampstead, who gave the alarm.

ANDES EXPEDITION

Maths master Robin Bradford,

PRESIDENT —LIKE HIS FATHER

Estate agent and surveyor Mr. Sidney Spyer, of Finchley Road, on Tuesday became Hampstead Rotary Club's 33rd president 25 years after his father, the late Mr. George Spyer, held the club's highest honour.

A Rotarian since 1946, Mr. Spyer succeeds Councillor Bernard West, Hampstead's mayor.

Paying tribute to Mr. West, past president Mr. John Parkhurst said he had done the two jobs supremely well.

"It is nothing new for this club to have members who have become mayors," he added, "But I think it is unique in Rotary for a mayor to be president in the same year.

New avenues

"We are grateful to him for the tremendous effort he has put

Sensation: The Hampstead Garden Suburb *and* Golders Green News *reports the 1962 fire.*

Above and left: the aftermath of the 1962 fire, which destroyed most of the clubhouse and its contents.

Right: irons in the fire – members would shortly be getting new sets.

was thought the insurance would not cover the full cost of reinstatement. Thought would have to be given as to the best way to raise funds.

What the committee was saying was that the Club was under-insured. Interestingly, there was no comment subsequently in the minutes as to how this damaging situation had been allowed to come about.

The architect was appointed on 1 August and the local builder estimated a rebuilding cost of £36,000. Temporary buildings were hired, and the South Herts Club

offered to lend furniture – an offer that was accepted.

The general committee was advised, on 22 September, that the Club was overdrawn and subscriptions would have to increase in 1963. It was suggested that the committee and officers should continue until the clubhouse had been rebuilt and this proposition was agreed at an EGM held on 3 November.

The house committee decided to restrict the Men's Dinner to a maximum of 50 because of the limited accommodation available and the meal, including wines, would cost £1.1.0.

A critical re-construction committee meeting took place on 25 October. The Club had put forward a claim to the insurers for £54,000, of which £6,000 had already been spent on fees, demolition and the removal of material after the fire, so theoretically there was £48,000 left for rebuilding. However, £6,000 of this was subject "to argument" with the insurers. Additionally, the insurance provided for £10,000 on the contents.

The architect had produced plans for a new 14,000 square foot building (against 8,000 square feet for the destroyed building) at an estimated cost of £100,000. Because of the under-insurance, it was decided to ask the architect to reduce the size of the building in order to lower the cost. The committee realised that the Club was going to have to find new sources of funds, and the alternatives considered were:

- Raise a mortgage.
- Issue 500 £50 bonds.
- Form a limited company.

Whatever method was adopted "it would involve members in considerably increased subscriptions". At the general committee meeting on 27 October, it was thought the Club could rebuild and furnish the new building for a cost of £75,000, which would result in the Club requiring a loan of up to £30,000 to cover the shortfall between the amount expected from the insurers and the building cost. (A fruit machine had been installed and it was hoped this would provide the Club with revenue!)

The reconstruction committee met on 6 November and instructed the architect to produce a plan:

1) "...utilizing the existing foundations... (but) redesigning the previous accommodation..."

2) As above but "incorporating a two-storey central area enlarged to cover the terrace areas. The total area of enlargement being approximately 2,000sq.ft. The second storey to be above the kitchens and to be for staff quarters. The front area to be used as an upstairs terrace but to be earmarked for a future extension."

On 24 November, it was reported that an on-account payment of £13,000 had been received from the insurers, which helped the Club's finances considerably.

Revised plans were examined at a meeting on 15 December. These required expenditure of between £15,000 and £20,000 in excess of the amount due under the Club's fire policy. The general committee agreed the final plans, which would have to be passed by the membership.

At the meeting on 9 February, it was recorded that Hornsey Council had passed the plans. Various quotations were considered for the rebuilding, and the one from Messrs J Willmott & Sons (Hornsey) Ltd (who had built the original building) was accepted for £52,880 with completion in 40 weeks (the maximum quote received was for £63,411).

An EGM was held on 16 February and it was agreed to proceed. It was revealed that the insurers had agreed to settle the claim for an overall amount of £56,607.19.9 The question of financing the balance was resolved with acceptance of a 10-year loan for £20,000 from the Club's bankers at 1% above bank base rate – but with a minimum of 5 ½% to apply. It is interesting to note that the total club income for 1962 was only £10,934).

The Architect reported that the building work was progressing well, and, by August 1963, the roof was about to be erected. The new clubhouse was completed in March 1964.

During the building work, the Club hired Portakabins to provide changing facilities. Lorna Peters remembered that, during the fiercely cold period, with much snow, which lasted from December 1962 through to March 1963, there were frequent burst pipes and hence no water supply to the temporary lavatories.

As they say, it never rains but it pours. The pro's shop was burnt down in a fire some months after the blaze that destroyed the clubhouse. Those members in the habit of keeping their clubs in the shop lost their equipment.

There were some lighter moments at this dark time. One member had been on a golfing holiday in Ireland at the time of the clubhouse conflagration and was furious that he

Spared from the flames: the board listing the Ladies' Honorary Secretaries.

was unable to obtain a new set of clubs, as most members had done by claiming up to £40 from the insurers.

HIGHGATE GOLF CLUB

Denewood Road,

N. 6.

27th December, 1957.

Dear Member,

BAR IMPROVEMENTS

The Committee have done their best to come to a satisfactory arrangement with the Brewers, but after careful consideration of the terms so far offered they have decided that it would be preferable to ask Members to lend the sum required (not exceeding £2,000) to pay for these improvements.

It is suggested that the loan should take the form of £10 Bonds issued at £9 and repayable over a 10 year period by deducting one tenth of the nominal value of the Bond from the annual subscription due from the Bondholder. To illustrate how the scheme will work, a Member taking one Bond will actually pay £9 and will have one pound deducted from his annual subscription each year for ten years commencing 1st January, 1959.

If any Bondholder ceases to be a Member before the end of the 10 year period the balance outstanding will be repaid within three months.

The Committee hope that the loan will be spread as widely as possible and that Members will assist the Club by taking up <u>at least one Bond</u>.

As it is desirable to put the work in hand at an early date I should be most grateful if you would complete the enclosed Form of Acceptance and return it to the Secretary not later than 31st January, 1958. I would add that in accordance with the decision of the Extraordinary General Meeting held on 19th October last the existing Bonds will all be repaid within the next three years.

Yours sincerely,

J. GEILS

Captain.

Tapping the members: the Captain writes outlining the 1957 bond scheme for financing improvements to the bar.

9 *MATTERS OF MEMBERSHIP*

Rules, rules, rules. Where would golf clubs be without them? In this chapter, we feature extracts from a pre-war set of strictures at Highgate Golf Club, then tackle the sometimes vexed question of the status of women members at the Club.

The 1935/36 "List of Members" includes various comments on etiquette, as well as other illuminating facts about life at the Club in those now so far-off days.

Slow Play

"The committee has received complaints of slow play, and of matches not exercising their right to pass other matches in front which have lost a clear hole. It is the duty of members, if delayed by matches ahead, to request to pass them (this should be done by sending a caddy ahead with a message to this effect). Should any match not give permission to pass before driving from the next tee, they should at once be reported to the Secretary. The committee take a serious view of this matter."

Clearly slow play had been a problem but the implication is that caddies were widely available, unlike today.

The bye-laws of the Club stated that "All caddies must be engaged and

Well I never...

In 1966, ladies were allowed to wear trousers in the clubhouse for the first time.

In December 1967, the committee decided by one vote not to obtain a television, but one was later hired. By the following July it was being claimed that this was the reason for a drop in the bar takings.

In 1968, gentlemen members were allowed to wear cravats instead of ties in the dining room.

Play on Good Friday was not allowed until 1959.

In 1946, it is likely that the club had the opportunity to buy the house behind the 15th tee, (which came with five acres of land) for a figure of approximately £15,000. The committee apparently considered this very seriously, with a view to turning the property into the clubhouse. It was decided not to proceed, possibly because of access problems. The price was also considered too high.

paid through the Caddymaster. Members are requested not to purchase balls from the caddies. Only the owner and his caddy may look for a lost ball.

"Servants of the Club are forbidden to receive gratuities from members. Any servant found guilty of a breach of this bye-law is liable to be dismissed".

Trenchant stuff. Today it seems unreasonable that employees should be penalised in this way.

"Children under the age of 12 are not allowed on the course or in the clubhouse."

Subscriptions were £10.10.0 for Gentlemen and £4.14.6 for Ladies and the total number of full men members was restricted to 350.

Mention is made of a loan of £4,500 obtained from the membership by the issue of £10 bonds, which were redeemed by way of a draw. The purpose of these funds was for improvements to the clubhouse and the course.

Lady members were allowed to play on Sundays after 1pm in winter and 2pm in summer but in mixed matches only. On Saturdays, lady members were allowed to play after 5pm (not very satisfactory in the winter!) but again only in mixed

SALLY WATTS

Canvas cures

TEE TIME

Canvas cures

AN UNUSUAL activity begins this week at the Working Men's College in Crowndale Road, Camden Town: a spontaneous painting workshop, held on Monday evenings and open to anyone who is interested. It is being run by Mrs Diana Halliday, who is also organising a series of seminars to start at the college next month, called Art Therapy Today.

Mrs Halliday, who lives in Rosecroft Avenue, Hampstead, was among the early members of the British Association of Art Therapists (BAAT), which was formed in 1964 and is sponsoring the seminars. Until recently she worked at an Ealing child guidance clinic, but now divides her time between private practice with patients and students, working as a tutor in Hertfordshire College of Art and Design, which has the only full-time art therapy course, and being a private painter at her studio in Church Row. Later this month she will run an advanced workshop at Camden Institute.

Art therapy began as a treatment procedure in the 1940s, and BAAT was formed in London to ensure a high standard of practice and establish appropriate salary structures.

Today it has 200 members, and the membership is "going up by leaps and bounds," says Diana Halliday. Inquiries are also received from abroad, where there are associate members. Part of BAAT's work involves inaugurating and approving training courses.

A note in one of its leaflets claims that therapists in art — also in music, dance and drama — are trained to higher standards than are occupational therapists; those practising in-art have secondary education until the age of 18, followed by four to seven years of full-time higher education.

Mrs Halliday explains that applicants well outnumber acceptances. She says that the long higher education is vital: "We are working in visual psychotherapy and training should be as high as possible. The art therapist has a one-to-one relationship with the patient, which is therefore a very personal one, involving a tremendous responsibility to ensure safe, understanding treatment."

But although she teaches and mounts courses, she herself has no orthodox training, for the simple reason that none was available when she began. Having had an art training, Mrs Halliday was working in Montreal in the 1940s, painting privately and also teaching, when a hospital surgeon invited the school where she taught to send a teacher to work with two post-operative patients. The venture was a success, and later she worked with art students suffering from exam stress.

"But there were no books or training courses—I had to find it all out from experience so my training was purely conceptual," she says.

Today's chairman of BAAT is Miss Diane Waller, of Northwood Road, Highgate, who is a tutor at Goldsmiths College as well as painting.

This form of therapy is used not only for psychiatric patients but in remedial and special education, as part of rehabilitation programme for people leaving and prisons, and to

TEE TIME

BENIGN September sunshine picks out the first changes of colour in the trees and encompasses the smooth, rolling greensward, the view across Hampstead Garden Suburb to St Jude's and the women golfers wheeling their trolleys over the last lap of the course as they return to base.

For this is Ladies' Day at Highgate Golf Club. In other words it is Wednesday, the important day of the week for a good proportion of the 100 or so women members who come here for a morning of golf followed by lunch, and then an afternoon of bridge followed by tea. And although this is their big day, for golf and for socialising, they also come at plenty of other times. But not on Saturday or Sunday mornings, these times being sacrosanct to the male members.

You might think that ladies' days and men-only half-days are anachronisms at a time when equality is paramount. But private clubs are entitled to make their own rules in these matters. And the several women members I spoke to, all past captains, don't see it that way at all. Neither does the present captain, Mrs Ursula Poole, at whose home in Heatngate, Hampstead Garden Suburb, I met them.

Far from clamouring about discrimination, they are pleased with the progress made over the years, in golfing attitudes generally and at their own club, as well. Also, they point out that Highgate Golf Club, which was formed around the turn of the century, is really a men's club, run by men, with three times as many male members.

Women are associate members; they pay a lower subscription fee, have their own captain, committee and annual meeting. And should any little problem arise, the ladies' captain takes it up with the gentlemen's captain. And the men have the final word.

"Discrimination is going as more women take up golf," says Mrs Jean Thomson. "When I first played at Highgate we had to have a male player going round with us on Sunday afternoons, and once when none of the men was available, we had to have a little boy of 12."

His mother was one of the players, and if that child grew up with a superiority complex about himself and men in general, one could hardly blame him. Although still in force in the mid-1950s, this odd regulation has long since departed. In fact, the club is quite enlightened. It may not have reached the stage of two clubs cited by Mrs Connie Tilby, which are women's clubs run by women, but neither is it like the one near Liverpool where women are required to use the back entrance.

"I know—it happened to me," laments Mrs Tilby with feeling. Another thing that happened to her, this time at a club near Birmingham, was that she was not allowed to be served a drink on the terrace with her husband.

Highgate, however, does not go in for such idiosyncratic rules. And judging by the members I spoke to, they wisely believe in a policy of hastening slowly rather than of rocking the boat.

"We don't want a full frontal attack; better a process of attrition," comments Mrs Thomson, of Wood Vale, Muswell Hill.

"It's a question of whittling away," added Mrs Tilby, who used to live in Lanchester Road, Highgate, and is now at Totteridge. "We've only got to try and live a bit longer and it'll be all right."

Men these days are much less diehard, in the opinion of Mrs Norah Fletcher, of Lissenden Gardens, Highgate. "Mind you, it's taken 21 years. When I was captain in 1956 I had to discuss young business girls becoming members, and I spent two hours talking to four of the more diehard men."

As Mrs Fletcher is far from being mealy-mouthed, we can imagine that her captive audience men have had a faintly uncomfortable two hours. However, improvements crept in, based on the fact that so many women work outside the home that they can't play during the week, unless on summer evenings, and we need playing time at weekends. During Mrs Poole's captaincy, the women's Saturday playing times have increased, so that's another success.

As Mrs Fletcher reflects: "There are far more subtle ways of doing things than militancy."

Not only have attitudes to women changed, but attitudes in general. Mrs Tilby recalls how, after the old clubhouse burnt down in 1962, members substituted a nissen hut. One afternoon a fuse failed so the ladies sat in the nissen hut, wearing their mink coats and hats and playing bridge by the light of candles on the tables.

Ursula Poole thinks that "everyone should take up golf. It's a good game for women and there's a good age mix, from children to people in their 70's. And they all defend the £65 subscription fee (£80 for men) by insisting that there isn't just golf — on an 18-hole course—but social facilities too: bridge, a good bar and catering, a place to entertain friends. A number of women who have become widowed have found the club comes between them and loneliness.

The club can soon take over your life, says Mrs Poole. There's learning to play for beginners, matches, playing for your club, friendly matches, county meetings knock-outs — and of course bridge, which attracts 75 per cent of the women, though not the younger ones. Women members have their successes, too: Miss Annette O'Gorman, an Islington social worker, has just won the Middlesex ladies singles knock-out, and Miss Lorna Peters, a past secretary and captain, is secretary of the English Ladies Golf Association and president of Middlesex County.

But the small ratio of female members is continued among under-18s, with only two or three girls and 47 boys, many of them at Highgate School. Mrs Poole would like more girls to join. She thinks that for the very young, golf may be less attractive than a team game, but says an advantage is that you don't have to find a dozen other people before you can get a game; you can even enjoy it on your own.

When Ursula Poole—who will retire as ladies' captain next month and be succeeded by vice-captain Mrs Elsie Morton—joined the club 10 years ago, she had no knowledge of the game. When she applied to join, she was told she must be proposed and seconded by two people who knew her. And as she had just come to live in the area and knew no-one, this presented problems.

But she was keen enough to make inquiries and discover that a neighbour belonged, and also a friend's father-in-law. So she got in, and two years later proposed her husband—another sign of the changing times, as women have not always been able to propose men. Now she has a handicap of eight and has almost completed her year of office.

Jean Thomson's golf beginnings were quite different. Having been almost brought up on the Highgate course, where her mother was ladies' captain, she swore she'd never take it up: she'd had enough of carrying round her mother's bag. But the resolution didn't last, and she agrees with the others that "one can be a fantastic bore about golf."

Connie Tilby started playing to pass the time, more or less. Years ago she went to Freetown as a nursing sister, and was posted to the sister's bungalow, which happened to be on the golf course at Kaduna. So she sent an urgent request for clubs to the Army and Navy Stores in London. They replied in due course, saying they'd sent a brassie, three clubs and a putter, and adding conclusively: "This is all anybody could possibly need for Kaduna."

It was only when she came to Highgate that she really got involved, and was so keen that on Ladies' Day she made her daughter stay at junior school for loathsome dancing lessons.

These members reckon you can get reasonably good second-hand equipment that is moderately priced, and it's perfectly all right to wear jeans and sweaters, though you do also need waterproofs and golf shoes.

When I left the club the following day, after two meetings with them, it occurred to me that, far from discrimination, they are doing very nicely. For while the men are working hard in the City or wherever, here are their wives out on the course in this bonus September sunshine, having drinks and lunch with their friends, or engrossed in their beloved bridge. So who is being discriminated against?

● Ladies' Day players cover the last lap of Highgate golf course on their way back to the clubhouse. Left to right: Mrs Ursula Poole (captain), Mrs Jean Thomson (a past captain) and Mrs Elsie Morton (vice-captain).

Sounds of fiesta in Church Row

FOLK songs traditional and modern, from many parts of the world, come as overlaps into Hampstead for the new academic year—will be tutored by Miss Joy ing games of France, Swiss yodels, Spanish flamencos and songs from Israel, courses on poetry, novels, drama, a history of music and another on art, plus

Another view: The Express and News *reports on the women's game at Highgate in 1977.*

Well I never...

In the forties, a member called Ian Service lived in Sheldon Avenue, near the 5th tee. He had a dislike of pigeons, and would use his shotgun to deal with them. This used to annoy players teeing up to play the 5th. On at least one occasion, a fourball was bombarded with shot.

In October 1966, a member had a problem on the 2nd hole and ended up near the 18th green. The committee minutes noted: "A lengthy discussion took place following the recent incident when a member playing the 2nd hole in a somewhat oblique fashion attempted to play a shot from the area between the terrace and the 18th green over the clubhouse to the 2nd green with unfortunate results". A window had been smashed. The committee decided that, as this was unlikely to happen again, there was no need make it out of bounds to the left of the 2nd fairway. The committee were wrong on this occasion, for, in a mixed foursomes competition in May 1969, the author drove from the 2nd tee on to the 18th green. This time there were no unfortunate results, apart from his pairing completing the hole with 9 shots, the 3rd being over the clubhouse and on to the 5th green.

matches. Otherwise, ladies were not permitted to play on Saturdays or on bank holidays.

Restrictions for ladies were still in place in 1970. The committee received a letter from a member saying it was unreasonable that ladies could not tee off on Saturdays until late in the afternoon. A move to extend their starting times was rejected. This question was again raised at the 1979 AGM, and from the floor the comment came that any relaxation would bring into question the level of ladies' subscriptions and in any event the "ladies do not support the bar" – to which the Captain replied "this was not a drinking club".

(In September 1971, a member, Professor Brant, had suggested that the men's bar "was archaic and should be abandoned" but this comment resulted in no reaction from the committee and no action was taken in this connection until 30 years had passed).

THE LADIES SECTION AND THE FULL MEMBERSHIP QUESTION

When the East Finchley Club, precursor of Highgate Golf Club, was formed in 1893, there was a separate Ladies section, and this continued when the Club moved from East Finchley to Highgate in 1904. As was general practice at that time, the lady members comprised mainly the wives and daughters of the men members, but, over the years, an increasing number of independent ladies joined.

The administration of the Club remained very much under the control of the men members; the ladies had few rights and had very restricted playing times.

Over the years – most markedly after the Second World War – certain ladies attempted to improve the basis of their membership, and, over time their playing times slowly improved. An article that appeared in the local newspaper *The Express and News* in September 1977 gives an interesting view of the situation of the ladies at that time (see page 127).

It was proposed in March 1983 that the Lady Captain should sit on the general committee, and this was agreed at the AGM later that month. The subject of the ladies' voting rights was also considered. At this time, there were 448 men members (including 65 full USA members) in all categories and 132 ladies.

At the AGM in March 1988, the chairman, Bill Jack, suggested that members should consider the proposition that ladies should be

Well I never . .

In 1978, the cost of the Sunday lunch was increased to £2.45.

The notion of building a squash court was raised in 1980 but not pursued.

In April 1978, the cost of the monthly medal was increased from 25p to 50p.

In 1979, the Club agreed that the Economist *magazine would be permitted to land a helicopter on the course every Thursday for the purpose of taking its next edition to the printers at Crawley in Sussex. This produced income but was subject to taxation. Some members did not agree with the principle of a helicopter landing on the course, but in practice the inconvenience was minimal. This continued until 1983.*

At a committee meeting in November 1962, it was noted that the Ladies committee wished to dispense with the 'Auction Sweepstake' for the mixed foursomes, and this was agreed.

The Club bought a piano for £250 in 1977.

Well I never . .

At one time, many taxi drivers played at the club as green fee payers. Sometimes during the week, there might be as many as 10 taxis in the car park. Tim Chapman, who has been a member for over 50 years, remembers an occasion when he was entertaining a Swiss friend to a round of golf at Highgate. After the game, his friend was very impressed with the number of taxis in the car park that he believed were for customers, and thought he would be able to have one to take him to his hotel in the West End.

In April 1977, the club adopted "Chateau-de-May" at £2 per bottle as the Club claret. This was nothing to do with Fred May, who is pictured above in 2003 on the occasion of his 90th birthday celebrations at the Club.

allowed to attend and vote at the annual, and any other, meeting. A general discussion took place but no decision was reached.

At the September committee meeting, the matter was further discussed and it was decided to put to the male membership the proposition that lady members should have full voting rights. An EGM was arranged on 9 November 1988 to discuss and vote on this important matter. There were strong views on both sides of the argument, some being expressed quite forcibly.

Only 81 members, including those on the committee, attended the meeting, which indicated that the subject matter was not of overwhelming importance to most of the men members.

The chairman explained the rationale of the proposed changes and many members voiced their views for and against. When it came to the vote, the Captain and Secretary were asked to count the votes (by show of hands). They counted 40 in favour of granting extra rights to the ladies, with 38 against and 3 abstentions. There was a request for a recount, to which the Chairman agreed. There was then a head count, the result of which overturned the first vote, as there were fewer abstentions. There was then an immediate objection to the recount, as members who had originally abstained had voted. However, the chairman ruled that the changes had not been agreed.

The next stage in the saga came when the ladies committee wrote to the general committee expressing their views on the outcome of the EGM. Particular comment was made concerning the legal validity of he second vote. The Hon. Solicitor had already approached the Electoral Reform Society for their views on the position. They commented that in their view it was "morally reprehensible for a person to alter his vote", but that the second vote should stand even if flawed. It was decided that a further proposal would be put to the membership at a later date.

However, the committee's hand was forced, as early in March, before the AGM. A letter was received from a lady member threatening an injunction on the grounds that this meeting had not been properly convened (because the ladies had not been circulated). At this stage, the Club had already obtained counsel's opinion whose view was that the first vote at the EGM should stand. The AGM was postponed so the legal position could be clarified.

The committee obtained further advice from a second counsel, whose opinion endorsed that already obtained – that the first vote counted. Therefore, the ladies had, in fact, had full voting rights going back to the previous November.

The delayed AGM was held on 15 April, and notwithstanding the fact that some members had obtained an alternative, and contrary, counsel's opinion, the meeting proceeded (after a very full discussion) on the basis that the ladies had full voting rights. So, after 84 years of the Club's existence, the ladies achieved equal rights with the men.

POSTSCRIPT

The Ladies section had always been administered by its own committee, with its own competitions, and individual lady members took on the administrative burden. However, in the late 1990s, it became increasingly difficult to persuade individuals to take on the work. In September 2001, the then Ladies Secretary was coming to the end of her three-year tenure, and a replacement could not be found. The Lady Captain suggested to the general committee that the Ladies section should be disbanded, and this was approved in January 2002. A salaried assistant was duly appointed to work two days per week with the secretary/manager to help with the ladies' administration.

REFURBISHMENT OF THE CLUBHOUSE

The first recorded refurbishment of the clubhouse took place in 1925, just in time for the first fire, which occurred the following year.

Thirty years later, the subject of refurbishment arose again, and the Captain's letter dated October 1957 to all members is interesting in that it covers many matters debated over the following decades. The work was carried out in 1958 – and lost in the 1962 fire.

❛ You will see from the enclosed notice that an EGM is to be held for the purpose of considering the committee's proposals for an extension of the present bar facilities in the clubhouse to include a 'mixed bar' and I would like to add a few words of explanation about these proposals.

Since the War, the trend on golf clubs all over the country has been to provide better, more attractive bar facilities open to both men and lady members. In doing so, these clubs have wisely tried to satisfy a demand created by changes in social habits and customs brought about by the War.

The committee at Highgate has, for years, been fully alive to the fact that the present men's bar, with only a service hatch to the mixed lounge, is inadequate, but plans for alteration have always been shelved because of shortage of working capital.

Your committee are of the opinion that adequate bar facilities will have to be provided sooner or later and that, with constantly rising prices, every year we delay means an increase in cost. They have, therefore asked Mr Frank Shaw to prepare plans for alterations which, if carried out, will, in the opinion of the committee, bring the following benefits:

1. The Club will have two bars in permanent use, which will cope adequately with all demands. The present men's bar will be brightened. It will be more private than it is now because the service hatch will be closed up and, as the bar area will be increased, members should be able to enjoy better service in greater comfort.

2. The addition of a mixed bar should lead to increased turnover, which will, over a period, defray the cost of the alterations.

3. As the serving counter in the new

mixed bar will in fact be an extension of the counter in the men's bar and both can be served by the same staff from the same central point, it is believed that, if the addition of a mixed bar results in an increase in labour costs, such increase will be less in proportion than the increase in turnover.

4. The opportunity will be taken to install better facilities for keeping draught beer and thus remove what has been a cause of complaint for years.

Tenders received from contractors indicate that the cost of the alterations will be in the neighbourhood of £1,950. In that figure, however, there is a sum of £300 allowed for unforeseen contingencies, and if all goes well, the cost might be as low as £1,650.

The cost can be financed by a loan provided by Fullers, an old established and reputable firm of brewers. It would be repayable over a period of 10 years and would carry a nominal rate of interest of 2%. In return for the loan, Fullers would be appointed 'main brewers' to the Club, which would mean that they would supply all the usual brands of bottled beers and their own draught beer. They have assured me that the Club could stock any other brand of draught beer if the demands or complaints of members justified it, but, of course, it would only be fair to Fullers to give their draught beer a reasonable trial.

I would emphasise that this arrangement with Fullers would be entirely a gentleman's agreement. There is no question of the Club selling its independence merely to get this loan.

I would also like to assure you that the interests of the bondholders will not in any way be prejudiced by these new arrangements. The house and canteen results for the first six months of this year have been so good that, together with the income tax windfall already received, we have ample funds in reserve to meet the normal repayment of bonds.

Finally, I would like to record the committee's appreciation of the valuable services which Frank Shaw has so willingly given. His plans and sketches have been placed on the Club noticeboard so that you may have an opportunity of studying them before the meeting. **'**

For reasons unknown, the deal with the brewers did not go ahead and in order to obtain funds for the bar improvements £10 bonds were issued to members at a cost of £9, being

What a

The original Club suggestion book was destroyed in the 1962 fire, but an examination of the contents of the new book shows that many members have very bad handwriting. The subject matter and grammar often indicate that suggestions have been penned late at night. Here is a selection of gripes from members.

May 1971
"Will the committee please endeavour to improve the caddy situation and if necessary increase the caddy fee, bearing in mind [the] increased cost of living, fares etc. a minimum fee of £1 is not unreasonable."

An addendum was added:
"I was asked to sign this but declined, simply because there has apparently been no answer by action or verbally to serious suggestions previously made and the same situation will presumably occur."

September 1973
"That £50-£100 be spent on making the showers reasonably hygienic."

June 1974
"A strong recommendation that the

charge of 5p for a towel be restored."

February 1975
"Food: Egon Ronay plus. Clubhouse maintenance: full marks. Net, flags, handicap board, 4th tee, new bunker behind 5th tee: all excellent. Could a rake be provided for the last item please?"

There used to be a rule on the 6th tee that if a drive did not land over the road the player had to pick up the ball and drop it over the road with a penalty of one shot. A member wrote in 1975:

"I would like to suggest a change in the local rule which states that a ball hit from the 6th tee which does not cross the road must be picked up and dropped beyond the road for a penalty of one stroke.

"Not only is this rule anachronistic, illogical and unfair as it applies nowhere else on the course and the reason for its inception (i.e. balls going into the corner house on the right) has long ceased to exist. If a ball is slightly topped and stops just short of the road, a player has the chance of hitting a good second and getting on the green in three. The

suggestion!

present rule kills any chance of such a recovery. On the other hand, for example, a thoroughly bad shot that ends in the bushes beside the wire fence guarding the putting green suffers no disadvantage and is allowed to drop yards in advance of where the ball originally came to rest and on a relatively good lie.

"When I mentioned changing this rule to the Chairman of the greens committee... whereby you played the ball where it lies, or pick up and drop two club lengths from the hazard with a penalty of one stroke... his answer was that the rule would be changed over his dead body. I am sure that most of the members would be eager and willing to accept these terms."

The response from the committee in October 1975 was that "the committee has decided not to change the local rule". The matter was raised again two years later, and subsequently this most unusual local rule was cancelled.

March 1981
"Why do we have to pay 80p for a large glass of sherry if a bottle costs us less than £2?

May 1983
"I suggest that the committee should consider the provision of hair drying equipment in the men's wash room. Now that the Club is in favour of greater intercourse (social) with the lady members, those men members with full heads of hair will want to look their best before venturing into the mixed bar."

The committee noted the suggestion.

July 1983
"Has the hair dryer (procurement) sub-committee had its inaugural meeting? If so what was the outcome?"

The response was that it was decided not to buy the equipment.

April 1984
"What about the hair dryer?"

August 1996
"How about a chemical loo installed at the bottom of the 10th – especially for our elderly ladies who need a convenience half way round (as well as for the Sunday morning drinkers!)."

repayable by a deduction of £1 from the members' subscription over the following 10 years.

In 1982, the committee felt it was time the interior of the building was modernised, and a local architect, Roy Fawden, was asked to produce some ideas. His plans were considered at various committee meetings and eventually a plan was put to the membership at an EGM in the autumn. This was rejected partly on cost grounds, but also because of the uncertainty caused by the imminent expiry of the lease on the land and of the reservoir.

In July 1984 a refurbishment committee was established. The minutes of its first meeting note that the architect member, Bill Jack, could not attend as his firm had just been awarded the prestigious Covent Garden project in which he was heavily involved. The committee met on various occasions and were asked over the months to consider the possibility of building a squash court, a sauna, a snooker room and also a separate bar for visitors. A more urgent matter concerned the rotten window frames and this work was carried out and funded by a levy of £50 per member.

In March 1986, the committee saw the plans produced for the refurbishment of the dining room and mixed lounge The cost of the options ranged between £25,000 and £82,000. The treasurer felt constrained to point out that the Club could not afford this level of expenditure without raising additional funds (it is interesting to note the total Club income for 1986 was £225,936 with expenditure of £226,773). In December, it was agreed to proceed with the work for a total cost of just under £40,000, to be funded in part by the recently introduced bond scheme, which had raised £30,000 to be repaid over 20 years. The EGM held the previous month had also agreed the committee were authorised to borrow up to £10,000 to be available for the building work. Not surprisingly at a time of high inflation, it was reported in July the next year that the refurbishment had exceeded the budget by £7,500.

In the year 2000, a major refurbishment of the clubhouse, including the staff accommodation, commenced. This was completed in 2003, on time and in budget. The total cost of the programme was £545,000, an investment that has given members an attractive clubhouse to serve them well into the start of HGC's second hundred years.

Taking cover: this new practice facility was opened in 1997.

Loyal line-up: the staff of Highgate Golf Club pictured in March 2003.

Back row: James Seisum, Derek Mason, Ronald Salt, Paul Bann, Leslie Judd, Maurice Soper Dyer, Russell King, Gavin Went, Nick Banks, Richard Andrews and Tony Lashmar.

Front row: Margaret Williams, Ian Jackson, Angela Bedford, Gordon Wilson, Angela Jackson, Robin Turner and Jimmy O'Connell.

APPENDIX A: Club Accounts

The report accompanying the 1915/16 accounts reveals the following information:

Subscriptions were £1,585, a reduction of £69 over the previous year (the effect of the Great War starting to bite).

Overall expenditure had increased from £2,208 to £2,362. Wages for staff working on the course had remained the same over 1914/15 at £637-17-9, but house wages had increased from £296 to £304 and the Secretary's salary remained constant at £120 per annum. The wages of the professional and caddymaster had risen from £82 to £85. The stable expenses had increased from £73 to £131 and the cost of hiring horses (for grass cutting) had gone up from £29 to £38. Both these items were affected by the war, with the army acquiring large numbers of horses for military use. Overall the accounts reveal a loss for the year of £255.

In 1920/21 the accounts reveal that income had increased to £4,064 but the loss on the year's activities was £930. Presumably the Club was still suffering from the effect of the War.

By 1934, there were 683 members in all categories and the club was prospering. However, income was now only £5,631 – not a huge increase on 14 years earlier, and reflecting the economic conditions at the time.

The accounts of that year reveal that there was a lack of support for the catering facilities. To quote: "During the year, the experiment of providing lower-priced meals on an à la carte basis was tried, in the expectation that consumption would be increased. The anticipated support was not forthcoming and the result has not proved successful."

Mrs Betty Whipple remembered that, at that time, there was a fairly constant waitress service and the steward was always pleased to provide meals after an evening game. Dances were held in the men's bar. Table tennis was played in the ladies' lounge, usually on Sunday evenings up to 11 o'clock. Men played by invitation. Occasionally there was country dancing, with music provided by a wind-up gramophone.

Apart from spending money on the course, the committee also extended the clubhouse by building a porch to the dressing room, recurtaining the lounge and dining room, and improving the seats in the bar. Improvements were also made in the kitchen.

The accounts still show stable expenses, so the Club was not yet fully mechanised.

1940

The total membership was now 708 with 312 full men members and 159 ladies. There are now no stable expenses but petroleum products cost £53.

Expenditure on allotments is shown at £31. As mentioned previously, these were again introduced, as in the First World War, so that members, particularly those without gardens, could grow their own vegetables.

The Club's income remained fairly static at £5,335, but a loss resulted of £506 (compared with a surplus of £184 the previous year) and it was at this stage that the Club approached the Church Commissioners to attempt (successfully) to obtain a reduction in the annual rent.

HIGHGATE GOLF CLUB.

Twelfth Annual Report of the Committee, and Statement of Accounts to 31st March, 1916 to be submitted to the General Meeting on the 27th May, 1916.

The Committee has the pleasure of submitting to the Members the Statement of Accounts to the 31st March, 1916, with the certificate of the Auditors thereon.

The expenditure in wages on the Course—£637—is the same as for last year. The total expenditure on the Course stands at £1,530 against £1,362 for 1914-15. The excess is made up of £36 in Materials, £35 on Upkeep of Plant, &c., £31 on Rates and Taxes, and £66 in Stable expenses due chiefly to the high price of corn and fodder.

The entrance fees and fees paid by visitors during the past five years are as follows :—

	1911-12	1912-13	1913-14	1914-15	1915-16
Entrance Fees ...	£214	£295	£273	£202	£185
Visitors' Fees ...	348	405	504	438	238

As compared with last year there is a loss of £200 under Visitors' Fees, while the profit in the Canteen shows a decrease of £158.

Under General Expenses economies have been effected in various directions, but the net result for the year is an excess of Expenditure over Income of £254 19s. 0d. It is thought that this will not appear unsatisfactory in view of the exceptional conditions of the present time. The Committee has considered it essential to maintain the Course at its usual standard.

A Roll of Honour, the gift of the Captain, showing the names of Members and sons of Members who have served or are now serving in H. M. Forces in the War, has been hung in the Club House.

The present membership of the Club is as follows :

317 Full Members (including 37 on Active Service).
  2 Honorary Members.
  1 University   do.
  4 Five-day Members.
14 Country   do.
21 Non-playing do.   Men.
  3 Waiting   do.
125 Lady   do.
33 Lady   do.   (Provisional)
18 Lady   do.   (Non-playing)
  4 Lady Waiting Members.
  1 Lady Honorary Member.
  2 Boy Members.
——
545

By Order of the Committee,

F. J. McLAUGHLIN,

Secretary.

23rd May, 1916.

Club accounts 1916.

HIGHGATE GOLF CLUB.

Sixteenth Annual Report of the Committee, and Statement of Accounts to 31st March, 1920, to be submitted to the General Meeting on the 29th May, 1920.

The Committee has the pleasure of submitting to the Members the Statement of Accounts to the 31st March, 1920, with the certificate of the Auditors thereon. Notwithstanding the substantial improvement in revenue the increase in wages, the cost of materials and general expenses have resulted in an adverse balance of £930 7s. 3d. in the Income and Expenditure Account; this balance would have been larger by £102 4s. but for the surplus resulting from the generous gift of the Members, who subscribed for the purpose of purchasing a Motor Mower, which has been of inestimable service, and the Committee again express their thanks to the donors.

Restoring that part of the course, which had been under hay, and necessary repairs, &c., to the Club House and buildings have proved costly.

Four new Greens have been made and in other directions the course has been considerably improved.

At an Extraordinary General Meeting held on the 10th January last, it was unanimously resolved that the annual subscription of Members paying £4 4s. should be raised to £5 5s., as from 1st April, 1920.

The Committee has pleasure in reporting that a further extension of the Lease from March, 1925, has been secured on very advantageous conditions, which carries the term up to March, 1932.

The new Lease has been granted to Mr. James Anderson, Sir Bignell Elliott, K.B.E., Mr. E. Horace Holme, and Mr. A. J. Marriott, who hold it in trust for the Club

The Committee again tender thanks to Mr. Blakey for the valuable services he has rendered the Club in the capacities of Honorary Secretary and Treasurer.

Some pictures and a handsome sideboard have been presented to the Club by Members during the past year.

The Captain and President in the year 1918, not having had the opportunity, owing to the War, of presenting the usual prizes connected with their respective offices, suggested to the Committee that their gift should take the form of a Victory Challenge Shield this year, which was gratefully accepted.

Special prizes have kindly been offered by a retiring Member of the Committee for the best five Cards returned in Stroke Competitions (see Club Notice Board).

There has been a very large influx of new Members, and the present Membership of the Club is as follows:—

        306 Full Members.
          3 Honorary Members.
          3 University Members.
          3 Five Day Members.
         12 Country Members.
         30 Non Playing Members (Men).
         59 Waiting Members.
        124 Lady Members.
         44 Lady Members (Provisional).
         27 Lady Members (Non Playing).
          2 Lady Honorary Members.
          2 Boy Members.

        615

By Order of the Committee.

E. HORACE HOLME,
Captain.

22nd May, 1920.

Club accounts 1920.

(1934)

-7-3-35 9326

HIGHGATE GOLF CLUB.

Thirtieth Annual Report of the Committee and Statement of Accounts to 31st March, 1934, to be submitted to the General Meeting on 12th May, 1934.

In reviewing the Statement of Accounts for the period just terminated, it will be noticed that the finances of the Club continue to be in a sound condition.

During the past year the experiment of providing lower priced meals on an *à la carte* system was tried, in the expectation that consumption would be increased : the anticipated support was not forthcoming, and the result has not proved successful.

The policy of the Committee has not been merely to conserve a heavy balance of income over expenditure, but rather to improve the playing value of the course and to keep it in as fine a condition as possible despite the hampering effects of the drought during the last twelve months and of potential damage by leather jackets, which has been practically nullified by intensive treatment so that the Greens are now showing a fine sole of grass.

The amenities of the Club-house have received attention—a Porch has been built at the entrance to the Dressing Rooms, the Lounge and Dining Room have been recurtained, improved seating accommodation placed in the Bar, and steps have been taken to improve the service in the Dining Room, and slight alterations have been made in the layout of the Kitchen to further this purpose.

A meeting of the Middlesex Golfing Alliance was held on 28th February and 7th March, and although the weather was bad on the first day, the general result was extremely successful, and it is hoped that more of these fixtures may be arranged in the future.

A considerable number of Members have joined the Alliance and represent the Club in the various competitions.

It is the very definite desire of the Committee to foster as far as possible a higher individual golfing standard amongst us, and they are consequently gratified to note that the entrances to competitions have been above the normal.

A new meeting has been inaugurated by our Captain—The Horns of Highgate—an open competition between the Old Cholmeleian Golfing Society and all Members of our Club. This match and that for the Australia Cup we regard as two of the important events in our Club year, and, as such, we trust will always be well supported. Mr. Douglas Robb has presented a Cup this year for a novel form of competition—"Holes up"—which has created keen interest, and we desire to tender him our thanks on your behalf.

The usual annual drawing of Bonds took place on 21st October, when 20 Bonds were drawn ; this leaves the Club liability under this heading at £1,000.

The Membership of the Club at 31st March, 1934, was as follows :—

GENTLEMEN.	LADIES.
312 Full Members	156 Full Members.
54 Five-Day Members.	34 Provisional Waiting Members.
55 Non-Playing Members	5 Non-Waiting Members.
17 Country Members.	8 Country Members.
4 University Members.	3 Girl Members.
9 Boy Members.	22 Non-Playing Members.
2 Hon. Life Members.	2 Hon. Life Members.

For the Committee,

R. D. BAIN,
Captain.

Club accounts 1934.

HIGHGATE GOLF CLUB.

Thirty-sixth Annual Report of the Committee and Statement of Accounts to 31st March, 1940, to be submitted to the General Meeting on 25th May, 1940.

The Committee presents the Report and Statement of Accounts for the year ending 31st March, 1940.

At the outbreak of war it was decided to suspend the Entrance Fee and to give special facilities for play to Members in H.M. Forces or engaged in war work, to discontinue Competitions, and also, where possible, to effect drastic economies ; during the winter the Men's Lounge was closed throughout the week with a consequent saving of heating and lighting : the Committee wishes to express thanks to the Members in foregoing part of the Club's amenities.

The Committee expresses its thanks to C. A. Broadhurst and Sir John Wallace for presenting Cups for the Members and Staff Competition ; to J. H. N. Peel for the donation of £5 for the Staff Competition ; and also to the President, Harry Knox, and Captain, J. M. Gilfillan, for two silver tankards. Thanks are again due to A. F. Potter for the presentation of a Cup for competition among long handicap players.

The result of the Club Competitions :—

THE PRESIDENT'S PRIZE, R. D. Knox and C. E. Palmer.
THE CAPTAIN'S PRIZE, R. D. Knox.
THE POTTER CUP, W. Gilroy.
THE CLUB PRIZE, R. D. Knox.
THE LYLE CUP, Graham Walker.
THE VETERAN'S CUP, W. Gilroy.
THE GOODFELLOW BOWL, C. D. Walker.
THE VICTORY SHIELD, A. Field.
THE HIGHGATE CUP, A. L. C. Laborde.
THE DRAGE PRIZE, W. A. Gray.
THE AUSTRALIA CUP, W. A. Gray, H.G.C. ; E. A. Finlay, A.G.C.
FINAL OF MEDALS (Seniors), R. D. Knox ; (Juniors) G. B. Curtis.
THE SCRATCH MEDAL, F. W. Barnes.
THE WHITSUN BOWL, L. J. G. Boldero.
" DAILY TELEGRAPH " COMPETITION (Seniors), E. B. Edmunds ; (Juniors) C. Gilbert Baker.
THE STAFF CUP, C. A. Broadhurst and J. Oakley.
MIXED FOURSOMES, Mr. and Mrs. F. W. Barnes.

I have to report with deep regret the deaths of T. C. Grimes, a former President ; Sir Walter Forrest ; F. J. S. Broad ; W. H. Idris ; W. T. W. Idris ; T. P. McNaught ; E. Burton Fiske ; Duncan Whitehouse ; W. Marsden ; W. T. Hunt, and Lieut-Commander G. F. Gardner, O.B.E., R.N.R.

The Membership of the Club on March 31st, 1940, was :—

GENTLEMEN.	LADIES.
312 Full Members	159 Full Lady Members.
49 Five-day Members.	20 Provisional Waiting Members.
69 Non-Playing Members.	10 Non-Waiting Members.
22 Country Members.	4 Country Members.
10 University Members.	6 Girl Members.
10 Boy Members.	31 Non-Playing Members.
3 Hon. Life Members.	3 Hon. Life Members.

For the Committee,

J. M. GILFILLAN,
Captain.

Club accounts 1940.

APPENDIX B: *Club Officers*

NB: *The destruction of records in the club fires has led to certain gaps in these entries.*

YEAR	MEN'S CAPTAIN	LADIES' CAPTAIN	PRESIDENT	SECRETARY
1904/05	J. Stewart	Mrs Chubb		Julius H. Moritz
1905/06	R.E. Dummett	Miss Blakelock		Julius H. Moritz
1906/07	J. Andersonit	Mrs Church	R. Dummett	Julius H. Moritz
1907/08	B. Boney	Miss Hall		F.J. McLaughlin
1908/09	E.H. Chubb	Mrs Malcolm		F.J. McLaughlin
1909/10	Dr A.E.H. Chilcott	Mrs Mudie		F.J. McLaughlin
1910/11		Miss B.H. Dyne		F.J. McLaughlin
1911/12		Mrs Harris Browne		F.J. McLaughlin
1912/13		Miss D. Wallace		F.J. McLaughlin
1913/14		Mrs Fitzgerald		F.J. McLaughlin
1914/15		Miss B.M. Dyne		F.J. McLaughlin
1915/16		Mrs Homfray		F.J. McLaughlin
1916/17	J. Munro			F.J. McLaughlin
1917/18		Mrs Fitzgerald		
1918/19				
1919/20		Mrs Colwell		H.S. Blakey (Acting Sec)
1920/21	E.H. Holme	Miss B.H. Dyne		M.S. Blakey (Hon. Sec & Treas)
1921/22	H.F. Keene OBE	Mrs Homfray	H. Wade	T.S.K. Fishwick (Sec. & Treas)
1922/23		Mrs Chapman		T.S.K. Fishwick
1923/24		Miss L. Johnson		Mrs W.S. Pain (Secretary)
1924/25	Frank Runcham	Miss E. Williams	Sir Percy Hurd MP	Mrs W.S. Pain
1925/26		Mrs Murray		Mrs W.S. Pain
1926/27		Mrs Sharpe		Mrs W.S. Pain
1927/28		Miss E. Gilfillan		Mrs W.S. Pain
1928/29		Mrs A. Thomson		Mrs W. S. Pain
1929/30		Mrs W. Smith		Mrs W.S. Pain
1930/31	G.C. Macmillan	Miss L.F. Johnson		Mrs W.S. Pain/Soutten MC
1931/32	G.C. Macmillan	Miss Birtwistle		Col. A.C. Soutten MC
1932/33	Dr R.D. Bain	Mrs Chapman		Col. A.C. Soutten MC
1933/34		Miss E.M. Reid		Col. A.C. Soutten MC
1934/35	G.P. Harding	Mrs F.W. Barnes	Dr. F. Shaw	Col. A.C. Soutten MC
1935/36	Peter Ferguson	Mrs Little	Sir Alexander M. Livingstone	Col. A.C. Soutten MC
1936/37	G.R. Harding (?)	Mrs Murray	Dr. F. Shaw	Col. A.C. Soutten MC
1937/38	W.A. Fray (?)	Lady Wallace		Col. A.C. Soutten MC
1938/39		Mrs N. Wilkinson		Col. A.C. Soutten MC
1939/40		Miss F. Challen	H. Knox (?)	Col. A.C. Soutten MC
1940/41	J.M. Gilfillan	Lady Wallace	H.C.J. Williams	Col. A.C. Soutten MC
1941/42	E.A. Mills	Lady Wallace	G. Macmillan	Col. A.C. Soutten MC
1942/43	E.A. Mills	Lady Wallace	Sir Robert Graham	Col. A.C. Soutten MC
1943/44	E.A. Mills	Lady Wallace	A.K. Turner	Col. A.C. Soutten MC
1944/45	S.A. Taylor	Lady Wallace	Sir Wilson Jameson	Col. A.C. Soutten MC
1945/46	S.A. Taylor	Lady Wallace	Sir John Wallace	Col. A.C. Soutten MC
1946/47	H. Colville	Lady Wallace	E.A. Mills	Col. A.C. Soutten MC
1947/48	J.R. Pullan	Mrs T.G. Buchanan	Peter Ferguson	Col. A.C. Soutten MC
1948/49	G.B. Curtis	Mrs L.G. Lancaster	C.E. Palmer	Col. A.C. Soutten MC
1949/50	G. Batchelor	Mrs Middleton	H.J. Clarke	Col. A.C. Soutten MC
1950/51	G.K. Cooper	Mrs G.K. Cooper	I.A. Robb	Lt. Col. H.D. Harvey
1951/52	L.G. Lancaster	Mrs P.G. Petch	J.A.J. Venmore	Lt. Col. H.D. Harvey
1952/53	F.S. Shaw	Mrs J.H. Watson	H. Bedale CBE	W/Cdr. L.L. Bray

YEAR	MEN'S CAPTAIN	LADIES' CAPTAIN	PRESIDENT	SECRETARY
1953/54	S.V. Sheppard	Mrs G. Batchelor	W.A. Gray	W/Cdr. L.L. Bray
1954/55	J.C. Wilkinson	Mrs G.A. Whipple	S.A. Taylor	W/Cdr. L.L. Bray
1955/56	D.L. Gough MC	Mrs J.R. Murray	Dr G.K. Cooper	W/Cdr. L.L. Bray
1956/57	N.V. Chamberlain	Mrs Fletcher	G.B. Curtis	E. Stace
1957/58	J. Geils	Mrs Klein	J.R. Pullan	E. Stace
1958/59	R. Foster CBE	Mrs Drybrough	L.G. Lancaster	E. Stace
1959/60	W.S.M. Betts	Mrs G.A. Whipple	G. Batchelor	E. Stace
1960/61	F.J. Ferguson	Mrs Fletcher	G.A. Whipple CBE	E. Stace
1961/62	J.M. Lancaster	Miss L.H. Peters	N.V. Chamberlain	E. Stace
1962/63	S.J. Belsham	Mrs A.R. Slyth	R. Foster CBE	J.B. Reid/ J.R. Adair
1963/64	S.J. Belsham	Mrs E.K. Foster	R. Foster CBE	J.R. Adair
1964/65	G.M. Hayward	Mrs R.B. Hoole	J.C. Wilkinson	J.R. Adair
1965/66	N.C. Weaver	Mrs W.D.W. Brooks	I.A. Robb	H.L. Messiter
1966/67	A.R. Slyth CB OBE	Mrs J.M. Scott	W.S.H. Betts	H.L. Messiter
1967/68	R.C. Rowland Clark	Mrs L.G. Lancaster	F.J. Ferguson	G.H. Daly
1968/69	H.H. Grey TD	Miss L.H. Peters	D.V. Johnson	G.H. Daly
1969/70	K. Howden	Mrs J.G.W. Tilby	W.H. Sparks	G.H. Daly
1970/71	K. Howden	Mrs P. Saunders	Sir Thomas Bennett	G.H. Daly
1971/72	J.R. Pullan	Mrs W. Bamberger	Sir Thomas Bennett	G.H. Daly
1972/73	R.D. Trayling	Mrs C.D. Parsons	Sir Thomas Bennett	G.H. Daly
1973/74	R.F.W. Grindal	Mrs T.A. Williams	Sir Thomas Bennett	G.H. Daly
1974/75	R.F.W. Grindal	Mrs R.H. Phillips	Sir W. Strath KCB	A.W.H. Bradstreet
1975/76	D.G. Jones	Mrs E.F. Hopson	G.M. Hayward	A.W.H. Bradstreet
1976/77	E.F Hopson	Mrs J.W. Thomson	G.M. Hayward	N.F. Lockyer
1977/78	J. Henry	Mrs U. Poole	T.A. Williams	N.F. Lockyer
1978/79	A. Long	Mrs E.M. Morton	T.A. Williams	N.F. Lockyer
1979/80	J. Salisse	Mrs J.E. Eccles	I. Wallace	G.A. Beach
1980/81	C.R. Ferry	Mrs M. Brant	D.P. Moloney	G.A. Beach
1981/82	M.R. Mcfee	Mrs H. Jones	D.P. Moloney	Maj. M.B. Richards
1982/83	M.C. Winn	Mrs I. Bispham	S.J. Besham	Maj. M.B. Richards
1983/84	J.S. Beer	Mrs J.S. Winn	C. Woodburn Bamberger	J. Hill
1984/85	T. Webster	Mrs M. Parfitt	F.G. Chapman	E.W. Seager
1985/86	J. Dunham/W. Jack	Mrs C. Marrazzi	J. Salisse	E.W. Seager
1986/87	J.J.R. Pollock	Mrs S.M. Chapman	J. Salisse	E.W. Seager/ S. Zuill
1987/88	M. Miller	Mrs E.M. Wilkins	D. Gwynne Jones	S. Zuill
1988/89	A.G.A. Pepper	Dr J. O'Riordan	J. Henry	S. Zuill
1989/90	P.B.A. Ridett	Mrs E. Lyons	J. Pollock	S. Zuill
1990/91	B. Brant	Mrs R. Bardner	J.J.R. Pollak	C. Manktelow
1991/92	B. Adams	Mrs M. Hill	E.G. Russell	C. Manktelow
1992/93	B. Burwash	Mrs S. Miller	E.G. Russell	C. Manktelow
1993/94	W. Jack	Mrs C. Duckworth	Lorna Peters	J. Lafford
1994/95	J. Thomas	Mrs A. Pollock	Lorna Peters	G. Wilson
1995/96	M. Hoskins	Miss P.M. Hone	T.M. Webster	G. Wilson
1996/97	J. Drew	Mrs J. Spencer	T.M. Webster	G. Wilson
1997/98	J. Radcliffe	Mrs H. Corsi	J.M. Chaumeton	G. Wilson
1998/99	R. Lane	Mrs H. Radcliffe	J.M. Chaumeton	G. Wilson
1999/00	N. Moore	Miss A. O'Gorman	P. Ridett	G. Wilson
2000/01	S. Morris	Mrs D. Dutton	P. Ridett	G. Wilson
2001/02	H. Minto	Mrs S. Licht	M. Pollock	G. Wilson
2002/03	J. Hall	Mrs S. Walsh	M. Pollock	G. Wilson
2003/04	D. Booth	Mrs B. Green	R. Riddell-Carre	N. Challis
2004/05	M. Hartley	Mrs C. Ross	R. Riddell-Carre	N. Challis

APPENDIX C: *Flora & Fauna*

FAUNA OF THE COURSE

Member Neville Jones writes:

As an open space, Highgate Golf Club and the surrounding gardens make an important site for wildlife of many species.

For birds it is important as a food source, and as a large nesting site, and there are many places that are havens from predators. The importance of these havens – hedges, undergrowth and the small copses such as the one at the angle of the 6th, 7th and 9th fairways, by the 11th tee and to the right of the 12th fairway – cannot be too strongly emphasised.

As far as species are concerned, the magpies, sparrows and crows are obvious to all, as are the periodic visits from Canada geese and the occasional mallards. Less obvious by sight, but detected by sound, are the green and great spotted woodpeckers and the jays. Other species are the black-headed gull, the wood pigeon and the occasional kestrel.

And now we come to other species of birds, some only recognised by the practised birdwatcher. Among species that I have seen are mistle thrushes, blackbirds, bullfinches, starlings, robins, wrens, linnets, blue tits, great tits and long-tailed tits, nuthatches and an occasional common gull.

In spring, the migrant swifts, house martens, willow and wood warblers and chiff chaffs add to the list.

When it comes to animal life, we are all aware of the grey squirrels and foxes but almost nothing else is seen.

One of the most difficult tasks for the greens committee and the greens staff is to effect an acceptable balance between our needs as golfers and the needs of the wildlife for food and protection. The destruction of their habitat to speed up our game is one cause of the overall decline of many wildlife numbers.

Lastly, let us not forget the many species of butterfly that can be seen in spring and summer. These include brimstones, orange-tips, speckled wood, peacock and an occasional unidentifiable fritillery and blue. They need all the nettles and flowers they can find.

HIGHGATE'S TREES

Member Bill Jack writes:

Trees give form to Highgate golf course and define the character we enjoy in the different seasons. Trees shape the holes, and, in some instances, individual trees and small clumps of trees directly affect play. We need therefore to look after our trees, and continuously plant for the future.

Trees grow old, are subject to disease and damage, and need constant management with a programme for succession and new planting. Whilst playing, it is natural for members to take the trees for granted as part of the scenery and not consider them in terms of the part they play in the design and appearance of the course. Does it occur to many of us what could be done through new planting to make Highgate even more attractive and interesting over the next 100 years?

Highgate is a small golf course. Normally one would expect a course to cover at least 120 acres, and most courses cover 150 acres or more. At Highgate we have little more than half that in an area with considerable changes in level, and several boundaries with residential development. It is a very tightly planned golf course. It is the trees that configure the holes and fortunately, although at the time the course was constructed the land was in agricultural use, it was historically a densely forested area so there are some very fine old trees giving maturity and character to the landscape of the course and its surroundings.

There are parts of Kenwood and Hampstead Heath where woodland, which has been there for centuries, indicates the type of natural ecology that would have been found in Bishops Wood. The woodland was deciduous and of a type known as 'oakwood'. Oak, ash, beech, hornbeam, birch and alder would have been the main species.

English oak is the natural climax, and we have several fine old specimens on the course, both in clumps and individual trees, that make a major contribution both to the landscape and to the layout of holes. A particularly fine specimen is on the 16th, part of the clump of oaks near the tee. Other species that are natural to the soil type and ecology make their own vital contribution. While some ornamental trees that are not indigenous have been introduced to the course, such as conifers, Lombardy poplars, and weeping willows, this should be done sparingly in future so that the species used in our tree-planting programme are predominantly native.

Trees are used in a number of ways in golf course design terms. They are used to screen boundaries, to reduce the visual impact of houses and roads bordering the course, to define individual holes and to provide a degree of separation between fairways. They can be used to contain or frame tees and greens; and on some holes they are located in a way that directly affects the way the hole is played. Trees also need to be planted as succession planting to provide continuity despite the inevitable losses, and to reinforce and sustain the existing tree pattern. All of these design aspects can be further developed on Highgate golf course.

Trees also make a contribution to habitats for wildlife, which is an important aspect of the course. Native trees in particular contribute to the local ecology and will thrive more readily than ornamental species.

Over the past 15 years or so, considerable attention has been paid to the management of the trees on the course after many decades of relative inactivity. In the mid-eighties a tree survey was carried out and successive greens committee Chairmen, along with the greens staff under Derek Mason, the Head Green Keeper, have carried out essential work on the tree programme. This includes attending to diseased trees, shaping trees where necessary, felling old trees or trees which threaten boundaries or which cut out too much light and sun from particular tees and greens, and planting a considerable number of small new trees.

Through their wide variation in form, foliage, seasonal colour, height and spread, trees need to be selected and planted to suit the particular design requirements. As I have mentioned, the majority should be native to the Highgate area in general and to the ecology of the golf course in particular. Among the species suitable are the following.

TALL TREES

English oak (*Quercus robur*). Can grow up to 100ft in height or more and also develop a wide spread greater than its height. Suits a heavy soil. A majestic tree and the natural climax of Highgate's ecology. Important to continue the succession planting that has been done on the 15th/16th holes and the 11th.

Ash (*Fraxinus excelsior*). Up to 100ft high. Fairly sparse foliage so seldom casts heavy shade. Fast growing. One of the most common trees found in oak woods.

Alder (*Alnus glutinosa*). Grows up to about 60ft in 60 years. A distinctive and elegant tree with dark foliage and rust-coloured catkins in spring. Suits a wet location. Historically found along streams and wet depressions in oak woods.

Beech (*Fagus sylvatica*). A tree commonly found mixed with oak woods in south-east England. Can grow to about 90ft in height in about 100 years. A stately tree, wide spreading, and with a foliage that is dense enough to inhibit understorey growth. It has lovely autumn colours.

Evergreen oak (*Quercus ilex*). Grows up to about 90ft with a wide spread and a soft, cloud-like form. Fairly slow growing and evergreen, with dense, dark-green foliage. It makes a good screening tree. This is an imported tree from the Mediterranean, but it has been with us for centuries and grows well with other oak wood species.

Grey poplar (*Populus canescens*). Can grow up to about 100ft in 60 years. Fast growing, with a distinctive grey down on the leaves. Likes a wet location.

White poplar (*Populus alba*). Similar in height to the grey poplar but with a white down beneath the leaves. It prefers a drier, heavier soil.

White willow (*Salix alba*). Prefers a wet site. More appropriate to Highgate than the weeping willow (*Salix Babylonica*) of which we have several on the course. Fast growing tree with a medium density foliage. Can grow up to 80ft in height in 40 years.

MEDIUM HEIGHT TREES

Silver Birch (*Betula pendula*). Native to oak wood forests. Suitable for growing in clumps rather than as individual trees. It can grow up to about 60ft in height. There are several clumps of birch trees on the course, beside the 5th green, along the 6th fairway, between the 15th and the 16th fairways, and along the 18th fairway, are examples. The silvery bark with distinctive markings, and the light,

feathery, pale-green foliage provide an ornamental quality. Can be very striking if grown against a background of dark foliage, such as evergreens.

Wild cherry (*Prunus avium*). Sometimes known as gean. Grows up to about 50ft in height. Dark bark and brilliant flowering in spring makes a wonderful display. Like the birch, it is best in clumps. There are several on the course including, in the recent planting, between the 15th and 16th fairways.

Hornbeam (*Carpinus betulus*). It can grow up to about 60ft in height. This is a splendid tree for the course. It has a rounded form, and has a very dense, twiggy branch formation that tends to grow upwards. Its foliage is pale green in spring, turning through mid-green to a bright russet in autumn. It is a hardy tree and can be planted to advantage either as individual trees, or in clumps, or along a boundary as visual screening. It is a native tree commonly found in oak woods. Examples on the course are next to the ditch near the 9th tee and beside the 14th tee.

Field maple (*Acer campestre*). Can grow to about 40ft in height, but normally about 20-30ft. It can also be used as a hedgerow tree, coppiced to give greater density. Has a dense, dark-green foliage with lovely pinkish-apricot colours in autumn. Can do well in low-lying moist areas. It is an essential medium-sized tree and very suitable for Highgate golf course.

Rowan (*Sorbus aucuparia*). A graceful tree with beautiful berries, which make a brilliant show in late summer and with clusters of white flowers in early summer. It has fine-textured foliage and should ideally be in clumps. It is very hardy and can be planted successfully on exposed sites, and also in confined areas. Very suitable for Highgate. Examples can be found on the course between the 15th and 16th fairways. It can grow up to about 25ft in height.

Whitebeam (*Sorbus aria*). Grows up to about 40ft in 80 years. Can be used for screening. It has a distinctive foliage that starts grey with white flowers in May and turns greener as the season advances, with lovely yellow autumn colours.

Yew (*Taxus baccata*). Well-known evergreen used also for hedging. Makes a dense screening tree with distinctive dark foliage. As a tree, it can grow up to about 30-40ft in a pyramid form.

SMALL TREES

Almond (*Prunus amygdales*). Although not a native British tree, it has been growing here for many centuries. Normally grows 20-25ft in height, with pink flowers in early spring. It has light foliage and is very adaptable to any type of soil. Best, however, in a not-too-moist location and in a sheltered position.

Blackthorn (*Prunus spinosa*). Also known as sloe, it is commonly found in oak woods. It has white, foamy flowers in early spring, and the fruit in September is striking. It can grow to about 15ft in height in 10 years, and is often found in hedgerows. It could make a good contribution to boundary screening. Very hardy to both wind and frost, and can grow under tall trees.

Crab apple (*Malus sylvestris*). There are many species of apple trees, but crab apple is the wild species native to Britain, which is often found on the edges of oak woods. Can be used in corners of the course. Very hardy to frost but best sheltered from wind. Can grow to 30ft in height and with a wide spread. It has a dense foliage and beautiful flowers in May.

Hawthorn (*Crataegus monogyna* and *Crataegus oxycantha*). There are several species that are commonly referred to as Hawthorn. It is very commonly found in hedgerows and as an oak wood shrubby tree. As a tree, it can grow up to 30ft in height. There are several examples on the course, for example between the 7th and 9th fairways. Tolerant of all types of soil but prefers drier locations. It is a dense, twiggy tree with strongly scented flowers in May and June.

Holly (*Ilex aquifolium*). Holly is very

prevalent in the Highgate area and an excellent native, evergreen tree, particularly for use as screening on boundaries. It can grow under deciduous trees but in a bush-like form. As a tree, it can grow up to about 40ft in 70 years. The foliage is dark green and dense with leathery leaves. Flowering takes place in June. Hollies are unisexual and therefore some of them do not have berries. New holly planting would ideally have berries that are not only useful as Christmas decoration but are much appreciated by birds in mid-winter. Holly is the most common British evergreen and is found abundantly in oak woods growing as an understorey below the oak canopy.

Hazel (*Corylus avellana*). A bush normally 10ft-15ft high commonly found in oak woods as understorey, like holly. Flowers in February/March and forms catkins. It can be coppiced to form a hedge, and could be used for boundary screening.

Trees are best planted when young – smaller trees are inexpensive and very good value for money. The trees and shrubs described above should form the backbone of future planting and would enhance further the quality of the course. Our centenary provides a wonderful opportunity for investing in trees and I hope members will be inspired to make a contribution to the tree-planting programme for future generations of golfers.

APPENDIX D: A Message from the Centenary Year Captains

Getting the message across: 2003-4 Captains David Booth and Benita Green (left) and 2004-5 Captains Cassie Ross and Mike Hartley.

Our Centenary is now upon us and we would like to encourage all members to share this important year with us. Details of golfing events and social functions for 2004 can be seen on the club website (www.highgategolfclub.freeserve.co.uk), together with Highgate Golf Club centenary merchandise. Following Highgate tradition, we have decided to have both golfing and social events to celebrate the occasion. We hope you will support them to ensure their success.

We would like to thank John Chaumeton for researching and writing, and Nick Kent for editing and producing, this history of the Club. We know our members will enjoy reading it.

Centenary events

Wednesday 31st December 2003	New Year's Eve Party at the Club
Thursday 1st January 2004	The first competition of the centenary year. New Year's Day Stableford. Bring a prize, win a prize
Saturday 14th February	Centenary Dinner at the Club 7.30 for 8.00pm Guest Speakers: Tony Lewis, John Uzielli (R&A)
Saturday 28th March	Captain's Drive In at 1pm and Centenary Photograph
Saturday 17th April	Captain's Wine and Restaurant Evening 7.30 for 8.00pm
Saturday 15th May	Centenary Match at Hampstead
Sunday 16th May	Centenary Match v Hampstead at Highgate
Tuesday 18th May	Centenary Inter-Club Match
Saturday 22nd May	Centenary Decades Event followed by tea
Saturday 26th June	Centenary Ball 7.30 for 8.00pm
Sunday 27th June	9-hole Cross Country Competition followed by tea
Saturday 24th July	Men's Centenary Medal
Sunday 25th July	Ladies Centenary Medal
Tuesday 27th July	Centenary Match at Fulwell
Sunday 3rd October	Match against the British Golf Collectors Society Hickories team
Saturday 11th December	Children's Christmas Party
Friday 31st December	Centenary Farewell New Year's Eve Party